THRIFT TO Fantasy

Home Textile Crafts of the 1930s – 1950s

ROSEMARY McLEOD

HarperCollins*Publishers*

I would like to thank the following people who gave me much valued help and encouragement as this project evolved: Tim Walker, Claire Regnault, my husband John Quilter, Paul Orsman, Sara McIntyre, Louis le Vaillant, Vita Cochran, Malcolm Harrison.

All items referred to in this book are from the author's collection, unless otherwise stated.

Published with the assistance of a grant from

National Library of New Zealand
Cataloguing-in-Publication Data
McLeod, Rosemary.
Thrift to fantasy : home textile crafts of
the 1930s-1950s / by Rosemary McLeod.
Includes bibliographical references.
ISBN 1-86950-509-3
1. Handicraft—New Zealand—History. I. Title.
746.0993—dc 22

First published 2005
HarperCollinsPublishers (New Zealand) Limited
P.O. Box 1, Auckland

ISBN 1 86950 509 3

Cover and internal text design and typesetting by Sarah Maxey Design, Wellington
Embroidered title on the cover by the author
Photography by Alan Knowles, with the exception of the following:
Sara McIntyre, pages 16, 53, 223, 266, 267, and photo of author on front flap
Krzysztof Pfeiffer, pages 102, 163, 166
Aaron Te One, The Dowse, page 262
Vita Cochran, pages 264, 265

Printed in China through Phoenix Offset, on 120gsm Woodfree

RIGHT: **1930s tea cosy worked in fabric scraps.**

OVERLEAF: **Detail of felt workbag, 1930s.**

Contents

one

Part One: Stitching time

LEFT: **Embroidered tea trolley cloth with crocheted edges made by my grandmother, probably 1930s.**

PREVIOUS PAGE LEFT: **Detail of workbag embroidered in raffia, 1930s–40s.**

PREVIOUS PAGE RIGHT: **Dressmaking patterns, 1940s.**

It isn't long since domesticity was a New Zealand woman's inevitable way of life. There was no choice.

Our mothers and grandmothers, and their grandmothers before them, stayed at home all their lives, running households that relied on the thrift, ingenuity and housewifely skills they had learned from their mothers to enable them to do more than just survive. The quality of their own families' lives depended on those skills in their turn, and in their handwork, these women revealed dreams and aspirations that were probably seldom realised.

Women were bound to be housewives; they were not expected to work for a living, and relatively few did after they reached marriageable age. They were expected to marry, have children, and to make their relationships with their families, and the creation of comfortable homes for them, the focus of their lives.

Domestic arts don't build monuments to their makers, and they don't create wealth. Many were repetitious and dull tasks, and no trace of them — cooking, sweeping floors, tending to children — can possibly survive in any tangible form. But needlework, fragile as it is, stands a chance. It is that needlework, and the other textile handwork completed by women in the domestic setting, that has led me on a journey of discovery in junk shops and auction rooms for the past 20 years. I believe those discoveries, easily dismissed as mere fragments of cloth, tell a story of our identity and also provide tangible evidence of our past beliefs and understanding of the world, in these two remote islands.

Detail of tea table cloth embroidered by my mother, 1940s – 50s.

In these troublous times, with fluctuating values and worldwide trade depression, the one sure thing that we can do, and be right in doing, is to guard our home life . . . Make it a vital force in the present time — the one solid rock in a world of shifting sands — the haven where we would be!

NURSE SPICER, *WOMAN'S MAGAZINE ANNUAL*, 1933

In this book I am concentrating on the recent past, the 1930s through to the 1950s, a time when we were exploring what it meant to be New Zealanders, while still being deeply and actively tied to Great Britain. Beliefs held then still hold true today for many people; women's handcrafts gave them expression.

The women who came before us were expected to sew; they had to dress themselves and their families in a time when few people could afford to buy what they were capable of making. For some women this work may have been unwelcome drudgery, but for others it was an opportunity to express themselves with the only means readily at hand — a needle, some thread, a piece of scrap fabric. The work they did has survived mostly by chance, and it has left a tangible, intensely feminine record of those women and their time.

Women today have an uneasy relationship with that past; it seems truly like a foreign country, and those domestic preoccupations seem to them to be evidence of nothing more than stultifying and limited lives. The cottage and folk traditions of the recent past may even seem embarrassing; we are better educated than our grandmothers, we travel the world, and we expect to work on equal terms with men. Part of that expectation has meant that many women have abandoned 'feminine' crafts as being unworthy; they see femininity itself as trivialising women and our serious aspirations.

Yet I think the handwork of those women invites us to ask whether theirs was truly inferior to the culture of male enterprise, or rather a parallel culture that should be viewed as important in itself. In agreeing to deny its worth we are denying the sense of challenge that many women faced in making the best of their circumscribed world, and their successes; we are accepting that the male world outside the home, with its more measurable successes (money, status) is in itself more valid and legitimate.

OVERLEAF: **I look on this afghan crocheted rug as a kind of small masterpiece. I remember my grandmother Lucy making it during the 1950s, and then putting it aside in her bedroom for a long time before she would use it. What makes it so successful is the small size of each square (6cm x 7cm), the neatness of her work, and her careful, even use of colour. My Aunt Barbara took the rug when my grandmother died, and when she died, in her turn, I flew to Gisborne to look for it. It is one of my favourite things; it reminds me of an old piece of millefiori glass.**

We sell the women of the recent past short, surely, when we dismiss the worlds they made within the four walls of their homes, along with the domestic textile crafts they practised. They did not believe their lives were insignificant; they would not appreciate being patronised by people whose values they might question in their turn. The recurring imagery employed in their handwork, moreover, and the range of objects they made, are a record unlike any other of ordinary women's lives, and the values that were important to them. These women did not set out to make history themselves, but their handwork did.

It seems to me that in the 1930s, '40s and '50s, the last great period of domestic handcrafts and making do, women in New Zealand were asking two questions as they stitched: Who are we? And where are we?

These were questions my own family was asking, and the answers they gave still explain a good deal about us all at the start of the 21st century.

The oldest New Zealand folk-art item I can trace in my family is a jointed wooden doll in the Akaroa Museum. It was made by the ship's carpenter on the *Comte de Paris* for the Breitmeyer children, who emigrated here with their parents in 1840.

Catherine Breitmeyer, who was then a small child, was my great-great-grandmother. She belonged to one of the group of German families on that ship of French emigrants which, according to family legend, narrowly missed claiming New Zealand as a French colony. She arrived when the Treaty of Waitangi had just been signed, and I like to think that she played with the doll, which must have first belonged to the older children in her family who also made the voyage.

Most people don't know there were Germans on that ship. They settled at first at a place that came to be called German Bay, where I've read that my great-great-great-grand-father Johannes, a shoemaker from Pfalz-Rhineland, opened a small inn. At the time of World War I the name of the bay was changed; all mention of Germany was erased, and with it a historic marker for my family, who, like other people of German descent, began to describe themselves as having come from Alsace-Lorraine, a territory long disputed with France. This was not quite the case. The region had once been part of Bavaria, but France had claimed the part where the Breitmeyers came from between 1790 and 1812, before it again reverted to German control.

There is a lost snapshot of my grandmother, Lucy, dressed up and standing stiffly in a male cousin's army uniform at Akaroa at the time of World War I. She seems oblivious, as she tries to stifle her laughter, to the fact that he was possibly about to kill his — and her — own relations. It's easy to see from this how memory can be altered, fade and be lost, and the same applies more literally to material things.

For many years a sacking-backed rag rug made by Lucy's mother, my great-grandmother Alice Street, lay on the floor in a Tinui hall for people to wipe their feet on. I remember it being mostly black, orange and pink, popular colours in such handwork from Victorian times through to the 1920s and '30s. It would have been made from shreds of her large family's woollen clothing.

After her long lifetime of making handwork, only Alice's apron workbag, which my grandmother gave me, now survives. Everything she made, apart from that, has vanished. That old workbag is a bit like the smattering of German words my grandmother had learned at Alice's knee, a fragile trace of something distant and elusive, like a few bars of music you once heard a long time ago.

LEFT: **Wedding photograph of my great-grandmother Alice Pawson and her husband George Street, 1890s.**

ABOVE: **My great-grandmother Alice made and wore this floral patterned apron/workbag at the end of the 19th century, when she married and had her first child. The apron was designed to hold a piece of knitting or embroidery; her hands could be easily freed for other tasks while it was tied around her waist. When she took the apron off, the top folded into the bag, and it became a workbag with gathers that could be tightened to stop her handwork falling out. My great-grandmother enjoyed making handcrafts, and my grandmother kept this as a memory of her. I suspect the fabric, floral with birds, was curtain material; its colouring and design style suggests that it is late Victorian.**

Two workbags made by my mother from pieces of curtain fabric, 1940s–50s.

One of my older cousins did have a patchwork quilt Alice made, but it was destroyed by a son who used it as a grease rag for his motorbike. Stories like this about old textiles are common; they just look like rags to people who don't understand them, and that explains why so much of such handwork doesn't survive.

In defiance of that, I've kept things made by women in my family, and also moved on to collecting work by women who were strangers to us. They seemed to be telling the same unconscious stories, and in a strange way, they are part of my relationship with my own family, as well as a story about colonisation and the development of the unique culture evolving in this country.

Textiles are frustrating to collect. They are fragile; they stain; they develop rust marks; they fray, and tear, and rot, and then get thrown away. If you use them, they deteriorate, and they are lost to the future; yet if you merely store them, you don't fully enjoy the pleasure of possession. That's probably why they've not been a popular thing to collect; antique furniture and fine china are more sensible, usable and durable investments.

To an extent, I think textile handcrafts have also suffered from being women's work; that's long been a way of dismissing the idea of value even among women themselves. And then again, few pieces of this sort of work are signed. We value signatures because we can more readily assign value — and high prices — to them.

There are reasons why women did not sign their handwork, though. They were socially defined at this time by their marriages, described by and addressed by their husbands' names — my great-aunt Mary, for example, was Mrs Ivan Cripps — and their wider world was run by men.

Whose name would they sign, that being the case? They were also not expecting their work to be seen outside their homes, where everyone knew who made it; they did not need to distinguish their work from that of others. They probably didn't even expect it to last very long, but if it did, they probably expected their descendants would keep up an oral history about it.

There have been few books to guide me as I collected; domestic textile crafts of this period have lacked a story that could draw people into relating to them on a more than superficial level. They are so familiar to us that nobody has taken the time to consider what they may represent. It doesn't help that they fall into the category of crafts, either, rather than fine arts; crafts are looked on too often as a poor cousin to true creativity. Worse, they are made in a domestic context, so they don't belong in the consciously elevated tradition of craft objects which compete with the arts. If things are made to be useful, especially only within the home, and if they're made by ordinary housewives, we seem to have agreed that they can't be art.

Why not?

I did not deliberately set out to become a collector of these things, but when I was a child I did dream of becoming an archaeologist. Once I'd read about how people dug up the past and learned from it, I was hooked: archaeology was a combination of history and detective work, it involved treasure that was often beautiful; it was irresistible.

It's taken me years to realise this is what I effectively became, through collecting, without realising it. Journalism is a combination of history (as it is being made) and sometimes patient detective work. Digging for the past is what I've done in junk shops as a break from that work, and the themes I've seen emerging in the objects I've discovered have been a way of understanding the past through physical evidence, just as digging up a shard of pottery in the Middle East might be.

The New Zealand woman is generally considered to be the most like our own country-women. She is ultra-modern; she is Early Victorian — an interesting combination.

M. WINIFRED GUY, WOMAN'S MAGAZINE ANNUAL, 1934

I've learned about the history of domestic textile crafts from contemporary pattern and craft books and contemporary women's magazines. The way the projects are described and presented there explains what women were hoping to achieve, and even the long-obsolete purposes some mysterious pieces of handwork were created for. I've had to rely on family memories, too, to work out the significance of what I've seen.

I feel a kind of bond now with the makers, especially when I've been able to collect a number of pieces from the same — unnamed — woman from long ago. They become indicators of character and taste; a kind of tantalising, wordless message from someone you feel you half know.

The American experimental writer Gertrude Stein wrote a book with the provocative title *Everybody's Autobiography*, meaning that although we are all individuals, we share common experiences that connect us. In the same way, if your mother or mine made cloth dolls or patchwork quilts they

seem personal and imbued with specific memories; yet they were part of a far larger, and ancient, tradition. My collection is in that sense everybody's collection; it's about life in New Zealand in the recent past, and about everybody's families, to whom the things that women made, made sense.

Mine is a story of two distinct and very different families, as it happens, one of which was Kiwi Gothic, and one of which was imbued with cottage arts and cosy aspiration. That rift has been significant for me.

You can readily see the Kiwi Gothic tradition in New Zealand film, painting and literature. It's bleak, like a Vincent Ward film or a Ronald Hugh Morrieson novel; something scary seems to hover in the native bush, like the patch left on my father's family farm, or in lonely homesteads and townships where people turn inward on themselves.

Embroidered pincushion.

My mother's family, on the other hand, was more practical and sociable, as well as poorer. They belonged to a tradition, a way of looking at things, that never made it to literature or high art in this country. It seems to me it involved ordinary people, and as such, led inescapably to their own form of folk creativity. Her family's tradition was of valuing domesticity and cosiness, of making a Little England near Antarctica, of admiring the Royal Family, of upholding traditions of thrift and ingenuity as virtues, and of women's values and creativity taking centre stage in the home.

In my parents' lives, the mixture of Kiwi Gothic and cottage cosiness turned out to be a doomed experiment. The Kiwi Gothic world was male-driven, less accommodating to women's softening vision, and bleak. I'm not sure you could have had a matriarchy — my mother's family's style — in Kiwi Gothic Land, where men strode about with guns in the pig fern, taciturn, doing the Kiwi Male thing.

My father's family never approved of his marriage to my volatile and attractive mother, who came from a lower social class, and whose family style was so different from their own. She met my father when she was working in Woolworth's in Masterton, at the tobacco counter. He smoked. She flirted. They fell in love. Six weeks after they met, they married, and they seem not to have considered for a moment the possible wider repercussions of that decision for their families.

My mother had, as women did, a glory box full of her own embroidered tea cloths, tray and dressing-table sets, a trousseau to set up house with. These things had been waiting until she could play house with them in earnest, triumphantly hostessing afternoon tea parties, setting attractive trays of food for children who were sick in bed, decorating a marital bedroom with embroideries and flounces that could only make a man ill at ease, as was the style in the late 1940s. But she would never live the life she'd stitched in preparation for. Her copy of *The Book of Good Housekeeping*, so full of good advice on every conceivable aspect of domesticity, would never be translated into real married life.

We may think of the past in terms of happy marriages and parents who stayed together, but it was not always like that — if it ever was. My father's family did their best to break my parents' marriage up; they would not even let my mother's family enter their house the few memorable times they came to visit her; and they succeeded in separating my parents twice. The first was when I was born, despite the beautiful layette my mother had knitted and embroidered, and the second and final time was after a brief reconciliation between my parents, when I was five or six years old. The sad thing is neither of them remarried, and they remained fond of each other — even a little flirtatious — all their lives.

I guess their story says a lot about the time, when families could still get away with being tight and clannish and isolated, and when people were forced to conform to other peoples' expectations in a way that would seem intolerable today. That, too, is a part of the context in which domestic crafts were produced; they present a shared vision, a conformity which must once have seemed to offer collective safety. But that safety came at a price.

My grandmother made this plain baby's frock for my mother to wear just before the Depression began (my mother was born in 1926). It was possibly also worn later by her sister Barbara. This would have been sewn on my grandmother's treadle sewing machine, a wedding present (and effectively a dowry given by her parents) when she married. Although faded, this must have been a delicately patterned, abstract spotted fabric, consistent with fabric design of the time. The shape of the small dress is reminiscent of simple clothing patterns in a *Girl's Own Annual* from my grandmother's own childhood.

My grandmother looks to be about 12 in this undated photograph from around 1913. Her dress is obviously homemade, with substantial hem and seams to let out as she grew, as was customary for children's clothing at this time.

My mother did not believe herself to be inferior to the McLeods, whatever they thought about the relative status of her family. It would not have occurred to her that she might be truly inferior to anyone, and in an everyday sense her family's sense of class was defined in terms of industry more than by wealth; the Streets, her mother's family, took a dim view of anyone who was not industrious, whoever they were. My mother spoke bitterly about how her sisters-in-law, because of their perceived superior social position, were never manpowered during World War II as she had been, not long before her marriage. They were able to stay at home to look after their invalid mother, still a duty expected of women, while my mother had to work in a clothing factory, which she detested. What must have been especially galling was that they took no pride in that work, as she would have done. Women's magazines, with their clear messages about nest-building and beautifying, seem to have made little impact on them.

In fact, neither of my father's sisters, or their mother, would ever be in paid work. That wasn't unusual for women at that time; one of my aunts stayed at home, looking after the other family members, until they all died; the other married and had a large family. But the farm exercised over all of us — myself and my cousins — a kind of morbid and mythic charm as it slowly deteriorated. This partly Maori land on a 100-year lease was our stake in this country. It was our way of unlocking an understanding of it, and we took on board its Maori legends as well as our own — where the taniwha was, where the lost pa had been, the giant totara tree that had been spared by our sawmilling great-grandfather; where the catchment-board machinery had got stuck; and where the village of workers for my great-grandfather's sawmilling business had been, traceable under your feet in the deep moss of the bush.

I cannot imagine that a tea party was ever held at my father's home in my own or even my grandmother's lifetime, with best china and embroidered tea-trolley cloths on display. The house was not in a state of preparedness for visitors in my childhood; women did not hold sway there, or make key decisions, and the domestic arts were not in evidence. There were a good many guns, but I never saw a sewing machine.

The Street women, however, saw themselves emphatically as the equals of men; my Auntie Mary was proud she'd run her parents' farm single-handedly when her mother was widowed, and of the farm she later ran with her husband, as well as or better than any man. She and her sisters also practised textile crafts. I wonder whether a family's attitude to that practice is tied up in their beliefs in this way: why make them in a family which does not value women highly? Why not make them in a family in which women matter?

Visits to my father's farm were scary. There were long years, when I was a child, when the intensity of my father's family's feelings was such that, as with my mother's immediate family before me, they would not allow me to enter their gloomy house on the edge of the bush. With its dark blinds at permanent half-mast it hardly looked inviting in any case, but the Kiwi Gothic strain was heightened for me by all this adult play-acting and feuding, and probably made me lean towards admiration of the alternative. I admire, in hindsight,

the effort women put into making their homes hospitable and friendly, to children as well as adults. That doesn't seem to me to have been a small achievement, or even a small ambition. It speaks to me of respect for quality of life and for other human beings, and of fully making the best of things.

My mother's family were working people; market gardeners, small farmers who turned their hand to making things. It was not unusual for us to be bundled into a car together to drive past a family member's finished work and admire it: the lettering an uncle had placed just so on a new building; the parking area another uncle had levelled neatly with his grader; a cousin's elaborate wedding-cake-icing composition; another cousin's completed sewing project; an aunt's prized roses in bloom. There was collective pride in these achievements; we shared the sense that doing things well was important, whatever they were, and we reinforced our value to each other in this way.

Imagine a Kiwi Heathcliff out baying at the moon in the deep, dark bush, and his wife at home, sitting by the coal range with her tea cosy at hand; that encapsulates my two families' irreconcilable worlds. The cottage crafts are about being cheerful and welcoming. They are not introspective, but sharing; they make people smile, and they're intended to.

My mother had wanted nothing more as a young woman than to be a farmer's wife, as almost all the women in her own family were. She had grown up acquiring all the craft and housekeeping skills she would need for the married life she imagined she'd have, and she would have liked more children. That wasn't to happen. Fortunately for her she was able to return home to her mother, who would share the responsibility of looking after me. My grandmother became the anchor of my childhood, a patient and tolerant person who loved children in the same matter-of-fact, natural way as she cooked, crocheted or gardened.

Hers was the family I felt I belonged to; blunt, opinionated, loudly outspoken, honest, at times physically violent, clannish, minimally educated, unreflective, appreciators of dry wit. They encouraged me to laugh about my father's family's odd behaviour, helping to defuse it of its hurtfulness. More importantly, they accepted me without hesitation as one of them.

Society at that time did not readily allow for second chances; my mother was left alone with a well-dressed baby, and a husband whose finances were erratic and always precariously at the whim of his father. There was no domestic purposes benefit, or any form of welfare for her to subsist on. I was sent to boarding school when I was eight years old — my father was paying that debt off for many years after I left — and my mother did whatever work she could get.

For a while she was a housekeeper for wealthy women. None of those jobs lasted long, and the demands of her employers must inevitably have made her feel an even greater sense of failure about her own marriage than she already did. After all, they had the domestic life she had dreamed of. And it mustn't have been an easy thing to be the third generation of women in a family in domestic service; not when you were headstrong and good-looking.

My mother eventually left for the city, and ceased to be a small town and country woman. She embarked on many new and sometimes outrageous adventures. Yet throughout her short life she never ceased to make textile objects in the tradition of her

My mother, posing with her work-bag and knitting, in Wellington in the late 1950s.

Miniature felt gloves like these, made by my mother, were designed to cover the ends of knitting needles. They secured the knitting so it did not slide off.

My mother kept this magazine image of an idealised cottage interior, from the 1940s, until she died. It remained the sort of cosy cottage home she dreamed of creating.

mother, and her mother before that. She expressed something profound about her belief in her own self-worth in this way, as I see it, and it was the one area of her life where she met with nothing but success and pleasure.

I should think this is still common to keen practitioners of these crafts. Their skill is an island in their lives, a solace and an avenue to self-expression that might otherwise have no opportunity to surface. But it's also a skill that ties them to other people, a kind of sharing that weaves stories within families and communities. A textile object is history you can touch, which may become threadbare, but which can survive, given the chance. It may survive longer than you do.

My own earliest textile memory is the pocket of a green woollen dressing gown. My mother made it, embroidered a rabbit on the pocket, and closely stitched its fluffy tail in angora wool. She was proud of the imagination her needlework often showed, and this was a departure that elevated the simple garment into a small triumph.

I remember how pleasant it was to gently touch that white patch of softness, and to hear my mother talking about how she'd improvised the detail, knowing it would delight a child. Maybe that dressing gown was where my pleasure in such things really began.

There are printed fabrics I remember in particular from my childhood: the tiny floral pattern on a doll's frock; the large purple, black and white floral of one of my mother's full-skirted '50s dresses; the mixture of grey checks and pink rosebuds in one of my cotton school frocks, sewn on her treadle sewing machine; the curtains, printed with traditional English horse-riding scenes, that my mother once made in fit of aspiring to be English — a definite challenge in Masterton in the 1950s. Those fabrics form part of a visual diary in my memory, and a template for the way I've looked at colour and pattern ever since.

We could not afford to buy other forms of decorative art, and so our appreciation of it, our sense of what was fashionable and appropriate, was expressed mainly in the printed fabrics we selected and wore, made curtains from, or incorporated into textile craft work. When they wore out, those fabrics were of course recycled.

These were times — those I remember as a small child in the 1950s — when women dressed formally whenever they would be seen in public, in hats and gloves, carrying matching handbags. How they looked to the world mattered to my family, and in reality, few people who were not related to us ever entered our home. In this way the women in my family had distinct public and private visual identities: one corsetless, aproned and in mended clothes; the other immaculately groomed and corseted tightly into a public-life shape. The things they made reflected these two roles, mostly belonging to the world behind closed front doors where their beliefs about how home life should be staged were reflected in the things they made for displaying there.

I've come to see the huge variety of textile objects made by women like them, from fabric they had at hand, as a story that documents their preoccupations as clearly as contemporary literature, film or high-fashion photography did for women of higher education and social status. The humblest of the things they made record values, beliefs and images that had significance for their makers. Above all, they define a time when 'making do', not buying replacements, was an acknowledged virtue.

That tradition ended with the advent of the pill, and the opportunity for women to control their reproductive lives. Once women entered the paid work-force, as a result of that choice, home life became secondary for many of them. There was no need to make what they could afford to buy; they could earn their own money instead of depending on men. For women, as well as men, time became money.

The three decades before the pill — the '30s, '40s and '50s — were an era before popular interior decorators in women's magazines helped to fully standardise taste, before household appliances relieved the tedium of housewives' days, before passive television-watching took up leisure time, when imported goods were scarce and tightly controlled, and when people had less disposable income than they do today. Women still made what they couldn't afford to buy, or couldn't buy anyway because of shortages. Few women had much of a personal income, and a great many had none at all.

Life was far from easy for women, in a country that was, in European terms, barely a century old. This work shows how they maintained a steady course through terrifying world events, and found comfort in expressing shared beliefs that would have been gravely threatened by the changing and often scary reality of colonial life.

It's easy to be sentimental about the glamour of these decades in the Western world in general, based on visual records of fashion, film and decorative arts. In reality, they were deeply unglamorous for most people who lived them, struggling for security in a country without legends that applied to them, and without a history, before their arrival, that they knew much about.

Their handwork shows they were still scratching their mark on what was, to colonists, a new land a century after the Treaty of Waitangi. Women were more familiar with the plants and animals, place names, terrain and the last thousand years of history in their countries of origin than they were with the world Maori had created here over that time.

Maori were seen as another world in themselves, or perhaps at times merely an obstacle; we were endeavouring to make this country look like somewhere else, and be different from what it essentially was, during the three decades I see as central to my collection. Women showed this in the things they stitched, which were determinedly not of this place. Comfort lay in looking backwards, and outward from here, where they lived, to a place that seemed more real to them and which existed largely in their shared imagination. To speak of England was a little like speaking of heaven in my childhood; and so women making embroideries in New Zealand did not try to come to terms with what was staring them in the face when they looked beyond their own front gates. I suspect there was often scant comfort in that reality.

The three decades that interest me especially began with the New York stockmarket crash of 1929, which plunged the world into the Great Depression. My grandmother, Lucy, was a 28-year-old woman with two small daughters, my mother Joyce and my aunt Barbara. She would lose a baby, Lois, the following year, her husband would slowly become a virtual invalid, she would lose her home temporarily, and she would survive only because she was the daughter of a pioneer woman who had taught her domestic skills — sewing among them — on which she would now depend.

The women of the 1930s had World War I in their immediate past — it had ended only in 1918, not long before — and could well be married to returned servicemen, as both my grandmothers were; both my grandfathers had fought in France.

Many women had also been widowed by that war, had lost brothers, uncles and fathers, and would live to see their sons called up for service in the next. They had experienced another, lesser depression in the 1920s, they had survived the great influenza epidemic of 1918, and they had never been able to take security for granted. But the Great Depression would prove to be the defining challenge of their lives.

A popular New Zealand history of the Depression was called *The Sugarbag Years*; what women made with rough sacking sugar bags became a symbol both of their sewing ingenuity and the widespread poverty that called such an unpromising material into widespread use.

Women made rag rugs using sugar bags for backing; they made aprons; they made oven cloths, rag bags, laundry bags, and even — in my collection — a rough nightdress case, trimmed with scraps of floral curtain fabric.

New clothes — let alone other luxuries — would be few and far between. I own a pair of elegantly monogrammed peach satin bloomers which may have formed part of a 1930s bridal trousseau, and which have been mended, re-mended, and mended again with techniques of patching that are now a lost art. They are, in themselves, a record of what it means to have to stretch the last possible hours of wear out of a garment that was at first destined only for glamorous best. They are a reminder of why my family hoarded old garments, fearing a future without the ability to buy new things.

Between 1929 and 1932, the value of imported goods in New Zealand fell by just over 75 per cent, but the drop in value was far greater than those figures suggest, because of the decline in the value of New Zealand currency. We were broke.

Says Marie Dressler, pounding the table, 'If I weren't acting, I tell you what I'd be doing. I'd be making speeches to the people who are whinging about "the Depression"! I was out of work for nine years myself, but nobody knew it! Actors know what Depression means — and always have known. You don't catch them squawking. Mark my words, this Depression is going to make the rich folks richer, too. It's an excuse to economise on charity. Why can't people spend? I tell 'em shrouds haven't got any pockets!'

THE NZ TALKIES AND THEATRE, SEPTEMBER 1931

The lonely watcher re-entered the house, closing and barring the door. As she did so, two or three kakas flew screeching excitedly across the clearing, and a flock of parakeets, with loud, startled cries, flashed by the homestead. Her suspicions were now confirmed. She peered anxiously through the curtains drawn across the little window.Then her heart leapt into her throat. What was that?

'HUNTED, THE STORY OF A MAORI RAID'
BY GRACE SIMPSON, TALES OF PIONEER
WOMEN, 1939

New Zealand women had been buying goods and dress fabrics from English mail-order catalogues; many of the dressing-table sets, old dressing gowns and accessories, leftovers of the deceased estates of ordinary people which now fill antique shops, can be found illustrated on their pages. One such 1931 catalogue, in an indication of the growing impact of the Depression, announces that mail-order goods will no longer be consigned 'Cash on Delivery' to customers here. The *Oxendale & Co Summer Catalogue* says the company has suffered heavy losses trading with New Zealand women, after ordered goods were left unclaimed on arrival.

'In facing with patience and fortitude your present difficult and trying times,' the message begins, 'you will realise the increasing need for wisdom and economy in your buying of Dress and Household Goods.' And things were only to get worse. The vast majority of taxpaying New Zealanders earned, that year, less than five hundred pounds, and they were supporting families. They would soon have to take an across-the-board pay cut, and many would lose their jobs. No statistics were kept on unemployed women, but the widow's benefit in 1932, for a woman with one child, was just £73.12s a year.

The rate of marriage fell as incomes fell; there were 9817 marriages in 1931, for example, 1258 fewer than the year before. In 1936 there were 35,846 men unemployed or working on government relief projects, and 13,208 adult males reported they had no income at all. For women the figure was far more alarming; more than a quarter of a million adult women declared themselves to be totally without personal income. It did not occur to statisticians to ask how they survived.

Miniature embroidered pincushion.

Against this troubling background people still sought distraction, my family among them, in affordable popular entertainment at the movies. The child star Shirley Temple was idolised; Mickey Mouse and other Disney cartoons delighted both adults and children; Fred Astaire and Ginger Rogers danced, and their audience escaped with them into a fantasy world far from the reality of their mended stockings and knickers and recycled dresses, let alone the drastically slashed volume of imports that could have brought small, consoling luxuries into their lives. Despite our isolation, and many privations, we centred ourselves on our countries of origin, continuing to read English magazines and English literature, upholding English values.

In 1938–39, the first time such figures were compiled for *The New Zealand Official Yearbook*, 29,809 people paid to go to the movies; the average person went 18.5 times. This rate of attendance would rise after the war, and in 1955, New Zealand moviegoers ranked third in the world after the United States and Great Britain, on a percentage of population base.

Despite our economic troubles, we seem, in hindsight, to have been remarkably law-abiding. In 1931 there were, for example, 128 people convicted of offences against the person in the Supreme Court, another 78 for sexual offences, and four found guilty of murder. District courts found just one person guilty of rape. But the suicide rate jumped in the Depression years, for both men and women, and so did the rate of death and complications from illegal abortions.

The impact of the Depression caused New Zealanders to vote in the first Labour Government in 1938, with its radical welfare policies. That must have made people feel briefly optimistic about the future, despite the ominous signs of a coming war in Europe, but a year later World War II began.

There could be no doubt that where Great Britain went, we would follow. Social disruption began again, once more affecting ordinary households, as thousands of men, among them my father, left to fight the war in Europe.

Women were to lose sons and husbands, brothers, uncles, friends from 1939–45, just as they had in 1914–18. They could not count on either marital or financial stability.

Food and consumer goods were rationed during the war, and rationing continued for some time after it ended. A woman who could not make do would have had a cheerless existence, and there's plenty of evidence women continued with their handwork, in spite of shortages of materials. Women's magazines of the period are full of ideas to inspire them.

In my grandmother's home, as in many others, knitted garments that had worn out had long been carefully unpicked, and their now rippled wool was made into skeins for new garments. Clothes nobody could afford to replace were unpicked, sometimes turned inside out, and re-made, just as they had been a century earlier. And of course they were mended; women were experts at darning and patching.

At war's end, servicemen returned home to women who expected, and were expected, to provide nurturing homes for them. As in World War I, some men would return to children they barely knew, or had never seen — as happened in my grandfather McLeod's case. They may not have known their wives well, either. Like many others, my father's young parents had married and then, within a month, been parted by the war. I don't believe their hasty marriage was a happy one in the years ahead, any more than my own parents' would be. After both wars, many married couples must have found themselves changed for ever, but having to make the best of it.

Against this general background of disruption, grief and disappointment, women were urged in their magazines to make comfortable homes and rear children. The British-inspired philosophy of the stiff upper lip urged a stoic code of behaviour; a woman might have fears and insecurities, but they should be bravely covered over with a cheerful demeanour even if she was inwardly distressed. She should not complain. She had a duty to be a staunch wife and self-sacrificing mother. And in a sense she owed this to her husband, if he was a returned serviceman, because of what he'd endured. Women had to put themselves second in so many ways; maybe at least in their needlework they did not have to defer to others. The stolen time it took to complete a project could also be justified; it was for the family's benefit, and therefore unselfish.

The '50s would seem to be more settled times, in hindsight, than the obvious disruptions of the '30s and '40s; the war was over, though New Zealand troops now fought in Korea. But the country was divided in 1951 when watersiders struck for 151 turbulent days, halting vital farming exports. The Cold War, and fear of Communism, dominated the background to this decade, and so did anxiety about the possibility of atomic war. There was a major polio epidemic between 1952 and 1953 to contend with; 502 people were paralysed that year from the disease, and many were left permanently disabled. It would be some time before serious diseases could be controlled with confidence through antibiotics and wholesale vaccinations, and there were as yet few drugs to treat the mentally ill.

Despite such difficulties, New Zealand women were expected to carry on serenely making domestic life their priority, as if certainty of purpose was in itself a comfort and antidote to misfortune. Their textile projects continued to reflect an overwhelming nostalgia for the Britain so many had left behind, and which many more only imagined, and a determination to be cheerful.

In the new Queen Elizabeth II they had a role model of a young wife and mother, and with her coronation and royal tour of 1953–54, there was a resurgence of interest in royalty. It was a wonderful time to be part of the British Commonwealth, surely, while it was still intact. Who would have thought that loyalty to Mother England would ever end? Who would have thought that, one day soon, the churches would empty? Women stitched motifs and images that would soon form part of a past few people would recognise.

Women did not yet see themselves, when these objects were made, as victims of stunting social expectations or unreasonable constraints, if my family is anything to go by. They saw themselves as mistresses of their homes, deferring to their husbands, perhaps, but in charge of how the home — their world — was run and decorated.

My mother improvised this shoe bag from scraps of the striped chintz she chose as curtains for the kitchen in her state unit in the 1960s.

Tea trolley cloth embroidered by my grandmother, probably in the 1930s. My grandmother's embroidery was typically brighter than my mother's; they both used to crochet the edges of their work, but many women must have purchased ready-made crocheted edging instead.

They naturally gave up work when they married, if they had worked at all; a working woman was seen as a public reproach to her husband that he was not a good enough provider. But a single family income meant economising was a vital skill, especially when a couple had children. That responsibility typically fell to women, who handled the household budget.

Women's magazines stress that the ideal housewife was a multi-skilled and morally elevated being. Her duties involved childcare, cleaning, flower gardening and arranging, sewing, mending, laundering, ironing, decorating, cooking, nursing sick family members and budgeting. An article in the April 1960 copy of *Woman's Illustrated* describes the average housewife as a cook, schoolteacher, charwoman, waitress and chambermaid, dressmaker, gardener, private secretary, laundress, book-keeper, nanny and odd-job man. It estimated a wife was worth five ounces of gold a month in wages.

If she was a farmer's wife, a woman was also expected to share care of livestock and help with physical outdoor work. She bottled fruit and jams in season, preserved food, knitted and sewed her own and her children's clothes, as well as her husband's, kept hens to supply the family with eggs and rare chicken dinners, and often ran a vegetable garden and orchard for her household as well.

Some needlework of this time has images of Holland, and Dutch people in traditional costume. Since a good deal of that work predates the influx of Dutch immigrants after World War II, it suggests these images were designed to reflect a popularly held belief that Dutch housewives were models of domestic cleanliness and thrift, and to be emulated.

It's unlikely many ordinary New Zealand women measured up to the domestic ideals revealed in popular magazines and romantic fiction, let alone the demanding Dutch model, but they were ever present in the background of their lives, a marker against which they must have judged themselves. Women who had been in domestic service also had the background of the taskmasters they'd once worked for. Perhaps to mitigate against any anxiety about their own domestic perfection, they often chose whimsical motifs for their handwork, in a pretence that housekeeping was play.

It may be significant that in their textile projects during these three decades New Zealand women depicted themselves invariably as solitary figures — with the exception of a few images of courtship, sewn, perhaps, before they were married. Women almost never seem to appear together, or with children, in the imagery of their needlework, despite the reality of their situation as mothers. Family life may have been their invariable fate, but they saw themselves as individuals in spite of that, and perhaps especially in their daydreams.

It's also true that ordinary New Zealand women had spent a lot of time alone — with their children — in the first hundred years of colonisation. They had been left at remote homesteads while men worked to clear land, or travelled to get provisions. In the first half of the 20th century women were also alone during the two world wars, and during the Depression if male family members had to join public-works schemes based away from home.

This suggests women's textile crafts were practised not so much for the sake of the dutifully meek impression they might make on men, as some people have argued, but for women's own pleasure. Isolated women had nobody to impress but themselves. Perhaps, too, active creativity of this kind helped them to keep their minds off the loneliness and the fear that must have been a constant, unstated companion for many.

The conventional view of feminine domestic crafts, especially since the feminist movement of the '70s, insists they were a sign of submission to male expectations. I suspect the opposite is the case; that they were a positive and strong assertion of self. Women had to be capable, level-headed partners to their husbands in a pioneer society, and self-sufficient when they were alone. A vapid and submissive woman would never have survived pioneer — let alone Depression or wartime — hardships. Thrown back onto her own resources, she would have foundered.

Looking after embroidered hand-work takes skill; it has to be correctly laundered, starched, ironed, mended and stored. Women carried out these delicate, time-consuming tasks in the midst of demanding family lives. This suggests they valued such work for its own sake, and that the rituals associated with its use were important to them. Creating special handwork was, too, a way of elevating skills that were usually devoted to the mundane, of retaining a ceremonial aspect to lives that may have been mon-otonous and often comfortless. This, I suspect, was quite to one side of what men thought about it.

In any case, the few men embroidered by women in this period are hardly authority figures, who women would have struggled to please. They are docile, trapped in passively adoring postures as they gaze on a woman's flawless loveliness. Those images are very like the illustrations for romance stories in the magazines and popular light fiction women read avidly at this time, as well as the still photographs used to publicise popular romantic movies. The reality of marriage must often have come as a rude awakening.

Men have their sheds, where they express themselves through their hobbies with hammers, nails, wire — hard things. Women have needles and threads and sewing machines, and with these they still contrive today to make things that soften their world and blur the threats on its edges. Through the things they make, many still aspire to an ideal of domesticity, a safe haven for their families, and a means of self-expression that they can share with other women. But this is no longer as mainstream an occupation as it once was; working women have little time for such hobbies, and we've largely lost, as a society, appreciation for one-off, quirky, handmade things. Yet these traditions survive, and are undergoing a revival.

The time a woman spends at needlework is private, personal and quiet. Such time must have been especially precious to women when their domestic duties were all-consuming, and it may be why the very humblest of such projects could become cherished by themselves, their daughters and granddaughters, who can have little idea today of how and why they were made.

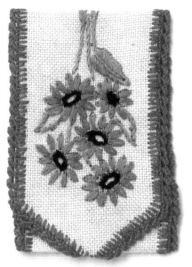

Miniature embroidered needle case, probably 1930s–40s, actual size.

Critics may say that many of these projects were not creatively original, that the patterns of the needlework exercises are commercial, but that is to misunderstand their character and purpose. These objects belong, as I see it, to European folk traditions, and many of their traditional design elements, as well as their techniques, illustrate that.

Real folk arts are not taught in schools; they are passed on from one woman to another, and from one generation to the next, through demonstration and example. They are the means of expression of ordinary people, like my family. Folk objects are made within traditions that are understood and appreciated by other members of that family or its wider folk culture; they are not designed to impress art dealers and patrons, but to please their makers in the privacy of their own lives. They are not made for money, and above all, they are almost all intended to have a practical use.

Displayed on this window seat is a range of embroidered cushion covers dating from the 1930s–50s. The patchwork quilt dates from the 1950s, as does the crocheted afghan rug. The rag floor rug, made from shredded garments, dates from the 1930s. It has a sacking back.

Felt toy mouse, actual size, probably 1930s.

publications that were sources of ideas, were by now essential for passing on the tradition, as people emigrated and lost their village contexts. Designers updated needlework and textile-craft projects and adapted them to contemporary taste, but they retain an inescapable sense of tradition.

These projects, and the magazines of the era which disseminated ideas for them, also reinforced links between Commonwealth countries and their shared histories. New Zealand women did not want to feel isolated; they must have enjoyed knowing they were making the same things as women in England, Canada, Rhodesia, Australia and South Africa.

Some '30s embroideries depict storybook, fantasy 18th-century characters. I expect this is because the 18th was the last century before the Industrial Revolution in Britain, when cottage crafts were still widely practised, when many people still lived in the countryside and retained their local costumes and customs.

That must have been a comforting time to look back on during the Depression. Many peoples' families, only a few generations earlier, had lived self-sufficient

If most textile projects of this era originated in magazines and commercial patterns, that does not disqualify them, as I see it, from being considered as part of that tradition. These publications were the preferred reading material of ordinary people at a time of universal literacy; they were produced for their benefit, and they reflect what interested them: royalty, romance, the behaviour of other people, their homes and gardens. Magazines, and the craft rural lives in their home countries, unaffected by concepts like international trade, banking and the stock exchange which were now causing them such hardship.

It seems to me that women's widespread exposure to affordable popular magazines, some of which they would keep hold of all their lives, was a vital factor in keeping these ideas and traditions alive. Such magazines are essentially aspirational. Through magazines, as photography slowly filled their pages, women saw domestic interiors photographed, and learned how more prosperous people, whom they would never socialise with, lived. Compared with film, in these days before television, magazines would have provided realistic and achievable inducement to domestic betterment. In New Zealand society there was more class mobility than there was in Britain and Europe, and so those dreams of betterment were seen to be possible.

In the past, when cottage and craft traditions thrived, women had limited access to different women's worlds unless they were in domestic service, which must also have influenced their expectations of home life. It certainly influenced my grandmother, and

probably her mother before her. Later, when my mother was a paid housekeeper, she also learned from wealthier women with different skills from those practised in her own family, and re-interpreted them into her own handwork. In my father's family, who did not have such contact, I saw no evidence of attempts at making the home attractive in the simple ways I was familiar with.

Some of the published patterns of the '30s, '40s and '50s — for tea cosies, especially — have now been in circulation for 70-odd years, and are still being made, evidence that they bypass mere fashion and have become as inherently timeless as other, more readily acknowledged folk-art objects.

It seems to me, though, that this 'upper end' of folk-art tradition, fed by printed patterns, has to be distinguished from the more naïve work whose imagery and execution originated with women themselves. Commercial pattern-based work is less instinctive, and the result is more out to impress. Like the modern craft and folk-art movements it may have its roots in necessity, but it lacks the freshness of innovation.

I like the way each of the textile objects I've collected is unique, whatever its origin; even when pieces are made from a commercial pattern, no colours are quite identical from one women's work to another's, skills vary enormously, and the chosen stitches are often different even when the same pattern is used. Each woman made her own decisions about how the final article would look. Each item says something about its anonymous maker's taste, and women made a deliberate choice about the needlework projects they chose to spend time on; the purchased designs must have seemed relevant to them.

My own preference is for the work that suggests serendipity, a kind of playful randomness of effect. Needlework may have the appearance of obsessive neatness and control, by its very nature, but I enjoy seeing a lack of perfection, even failure, because these homely objects have an honesty of purpose, whatever their origin, and perfection was not their goal. Each item is a finished accomplishment in the mind of its maker, even if others might find fault with it.

LEFT TO RIGHT: **My mother, aunt and grandmother in the 1940s. They are wearing print dresses which would later be recycled into patchwork, and edgings for sacking oven cloths.**

A toy dog, made from an old jacket, and with one button eye missing, is a toy that has succeeded in its purpose, it has been played with; a rag doll with a grubby stitched face has been loved by its small owner; nobody but the maker cares about the untidy back to a piece of embroidery, and if she doesn't care, why should we?

Some domestic textile objects — embroidered tea towels, table-cloths, doilies, aprons and dressing-table sets — were typically made when a young woman assembled linen for her glory box before she married, and it doesn't surprise me that many then lay unused in linen cupboards or bottom drawers until their makers died. What life could live up to such girlish dreams? What rowdy family would pause to appreciate such art?

My urge to collect really began, in part, because of curiosity, forbidden places and prohibitions. I lived, until I went to boarding school, at my grandmother's property on the outskirts of Masterton. This was a paradise for people who threw nothing potentially useful away — jam jars, string, rubber bands, buttons, hooks and eyes, glass marbles, the plastic animals out of cereal packets, Bournvita tins, white glass Marmite jars, old blankets — all were neatly stored in the expectation they'd have a future use.

During the Great Depression of the 1930s the property had been a modest berry farm with a small orchard that provided a bare subsistence living for my grandparents. The rickety sheds from that time survived still, in my childhood, spread out in the long grass on my grandmother's large, now overgrown section. They were padlocked shut, and filled with the junk she, my mother and my aunt accumulated. I was forbidden to enter the sheds. They became, as a result, an alluring paradise.

I could see old fabric through cracks in the walls (they were rough, unlined timber buildings that had never been painted, and had weathered to a silvery grey). They were, I knew, dresses the women in my family had worn years ago, which could never be thrown away because their fabric might be useful for a future sewing project. I played with the old buttons, which had been cut off

the garments and put away indoors for recycling in my grandmother's button box, but I longed to touch that fabric. It hinted at hidden worlds, a past just out of reach, stories I had not been told. Some of it ended up in pieces of my mother's patchwork.

One day the hoard of junk went to the tip, at my mother's exasperated insistence, and the old sheds were demolished. Furious, I salvaged my grandmother's *Girl's Own Annual*, from 1912, and refused to hand it over. I still have it. Its editor was Flora Klickmann, the author of many publications to do with domestic handcrafts at that time. She also wrote *The Little Girl's Sewing Book*, which my grandmother had as a young girl. I have her copy of that, too.

I seldom visited the farmhouse where my father lived, but it, too, had forbidden spaces whose charm was enhanced by their unfamiliarity. A room that had once been a small library was strewn with boxes of junk and fragments of material. I found one of the velvet bridesmaids' frocks from my parents' wedding there, cut up and made into a discarded cushion. Considering his family's attitude towards my mother, the gesture seemed appropriate.

I could never admit that I'd been into that room; visits had to be furtive and quick. Partly I had a craving to possess things I was told I could not have, but which nobody seemed to value; partly I felt that there was a story to be told here, too, among those boxes full of inanimate things, a story that the secretive adults in the house would not divulge. And I was probably right.

In a nearby paddock there was a half-wrecked old country schoolhouse, softened with patches of yellow and grey lichen. A stuffed pair of native crows stared back when you looked through the window, in a disintegrating glass case. There was an old, tiled washstand, too, with stencil-patterned tiles. My father claimed never to know where the shed key was, and many years later, the old schoolhouse finally disintegrated in a storm. Like my grandmother's sheds, it yielded eventually to chance and time, the enemies of all old things. And once again, I swept in to pick up a remnant of the past, the family's old homeopathic medicine chest.

My father's family hoarded things, I always felt, out of simple reluctance to let anyone else have them, and fear of losing track of its secrets. My mother's family hoarded for a more basic reason. It had experienced poverty, it admitted that, and feared that it would come again. This time — with lengths of string, old dresses, worn-out curtains neatly folded and tied with garden twine — it would be ready for it, as it had not been before.

For part of World War II my mother was manpowered into a clothing factory, but she also spent some time in the army. This tea cloth relates to that time; my mother had the staff of the New Zealand Army Personnel Wellington office of 1943–44 sign it, and she embroidered over their signatures. Finally she signed the autograph cloth with her own signature and army serial number. Quilts like these are related to 'friendship' quilts, which originated in 19th-century America, in which women each signed and embroidered a square, and the squares were then sewn together.

Some people collect out of a sense of nostalgia, a desire to evoke a comforting time that seems gentler than the present. I don't altogether trust nostalgia; it can be a sanitised form of history that blots out harsh reality and creates a fictional past I can't readily relate to. I have no reason to believe the past was any nicer than the present.

If I feel a certain nostalgia for fabrics of my childhood, and have carried home patchwork quilts just because they feature them, it's because I remember with what care and attention to detail the women in my family selected them. They didn't have much money, but with what little they had they relished the sense they were participating in a bigger world of elegance and glamour they knew existed somewhere. Certain abstract-patterned fabrics from the '50s take me back to dress and fabric shops where my mother agonised over which choices to make; certain combinations of pale yellow and grey remind me of my grand-mother, who favoured those colours.

I like the palettes of the past; colours are never quite the same when we try to recreate them; and I like patterned fabrics which reflect contemporary movements in decorative art. Old patchwork quilts are like an unknown family's compressed history: pyjamas, ball gowns, smart summer frocks, school dresses, shirts, thrown together and mixed into the harmonious whole the maker wished her family to be. They are a jumble of decorative traditions, past ceremonies and dreams.

I remember, when I find these things, the way the women in my family would keep offcuts from their dressmaking, and use them to trim an apron, or for patchwork. My family was typical of many in that no usable scrap was thrown away; it was kept in a sacking rag bag hanging behind the wash-house door until a project came along that would triumphantly transform it.

These may sound like nostalgic thoughts, but I also remember how hard women's lives were, that my family life wasn't idyllic, that having no money is no fun, and that domestic life didn't offer the women in my family the solace that women's magazines told them it should. I know they were not alone in this disappointment.

I see many of these pieces, then, as a wish for something better, a way of daydreaming about a life that would turn out well in the end, hopes for happy marriages and beautiful homes, and moments like the rapturous embraces in the magazine love stories my grandmother especially enjoyed. Maybe these objects were a bit like sacrificial offerings to fate; if you believed in the imagery, your wishes would come true. And maybe, too, women were realists; psychotherapy hadn't been invented, and there wasn't yet a language to describe their common problems. They just had to get on with it.

Although some pieces in my collection were made by my family, most were made by women whose names are lost. That doesn't deter me; it seems fitting that folk art, the art of the people, should be anonymous. It is the collective story objects tell about time and place that interests me, not necessarily the individual stories of the makers.

I have enjoyed collecting things many people have rather looked down on for the humble associations that link them to a less affluent past. That commonly held attitude has dissociated my collecting from competitiveness, and has given me the private pleasure of discovering what many people carelessly destroyed.

It was a surprise to me, when I curated the 'Thrift To Fantasy' exhibition for the Dowse in 2002, to discover that this country's museums had not yet identified domestic textile objects from this period as being suitable for collecting. But although it belongs to our relatively recent past, such material is becoming scarcer as older women die, and their houses are emptied.

All of my collection comes from within New Zealand; I have no reason to believe any of it originated elsewhere. Work like this was done in all Common-wealth countries where there was a strong English presence, no doubt, but I choose to think objects made in this country at this time became in themselves specific to the context in which they were made. Each Commonwealth country was

dealing with a different reality; each had its own race relations and cultural identity issues to address. To knit thatched-cottage tea cosies in New Zealand, for example, is an obvious comment on the maker's feelings about where she lived, as far as it's possible to be from England and its cottage traditions, and suggests to me a longing for a safe and probably mythical past far away. The numbers of cottage tea cosies in circulation still from the '30s through to the '50s suggests a collective homesickness and shared fantasy about the ideal.

What did such symbols represent to ordinary New Zealand families? How did they relate them to the appearance of their own timber homes with corrugated-iron roofs? And what did women make of native trees and plants when all their domestic handwork illustrated nothing but plants common in English gardens — hollyhocks, delphiniums, roses, formalised yew trees? Why did women choose not to embroider the natural world they saw around them? Why is Maori imagery so scarce? These seem highly relevant questions, considering that

Let us see about the background of the craft of embroidery. Taking into consideration the material necessary to produce it — cloth and thread, usually — I say it is then in close relation with life around the particular place where it is done, under the influence of what is happening round it, and the purpose it is servicing. The life of the people with its various facets will constitute the background of the craft, for through its material it will be a craft used for the purpose of decorating one's body, one's temple or one's house, and through these three different channels it will fluctuate with the forms of government and the life of its people. It is, then, essentially the art of the people!

'EMBROIDERY A LIVING ART' BY LOUISE HENDERSON, ART IN NEW ZEALAND, SEPTEMBER 1941

Magazines like this, featuring domestic textile projects of many kinds, were popular with women throughout the 1930s–50s.

domestic textile pieces were common in New Zealand homes, and were in everyday use. More than the historic utterances of politicians, I suspect the preponderance of some symbols, and the lack of others, tell a basic truth about who we are now, and who we used to be.

Thrift shops have, over time, partly satisfied my childhood yearning to rummage in my family's junk. Being things of little perceived value, objects like those I've collected have more often than not been sent to the tip by the makers' families, as the contents of my grandmothers' sheds eventually were. In thrift shops, where more charity-conscious families send them, they've been sold for trifling sums; the women selling them have not ascribed value to their own work, so why would they highly value similar work by strangers? Besides, it has always been customary for women to present samples of their handwork as gifts, bypassing the very idea of cash. Women resent paying for such things.

Between themselves, women knew the true human value of the time they had invested in their handwork, which made it more precious to the recipient, no doubt, than anything that could be bought in a shop. Time was, after all, a housewife's true luxury. It must have seemed indelicate, to older women working in junk shops, that such things should have a price tag at all. This probably also explains why, when handwork was traditionally offered at church bazaars for fundraising, prices charged were low, although items were newly made. And maybe that's also a reflection of the fact that housewives have always been unpaid, and became used to the idea that what they did had no commercial worth.

I expect many domestic textile objects became a genuine embarrassment to their makers' families, as they threw them out. As we've become more prosperous, we've become inclined to display high-status, streamlined objects in our homes, objects whose financial worth can easily be reckoned by strangers, and which conform to new ideals of a sophisticated, urban lifestyle.

Many working women today were reared in feminist homes, and such objects may seem to them to be an uncomfortable and embarrassing reminder of a fate they narrowly missed. They may well look on old knitted tea cosies and embroidered aprons as symbols of past servitude and dependence, or of limiting ideas of what it means to be female. But when the women in my family died, such objects were the very things I wanted most to keep.

My mother made this smocked flock nylon baby frock for me from a Paragon pattern in the early 1950s.

They carry their time with them, for one thing, but they also carry something of the hopes of the women who made them. When I touch them, the past I shared with them comes a little bit alive, even as my memories of their makers become hazy. The softness of textiles, the handmade nature of the objects, seems to me to be more personal than more traditionally highly valued possessions, and more intimate. They make the past seem real, and alive, and continuous.

My full collection of domestic textile objects spans more than a century, but my favourite pieces belong to the time of the older family members I remember. There was little money in any of their households, and it took commitment for women like them to find the means to make anything at all. Overshadowing everything were the great world events that shaped their time, and for ordinary people it must have felt like living on a fault line; they had to accept they could do little about random and huge misfortunes.

I haven't concentrated on refined needlework executed by women of relative wealth and leisure. Beautiful though it may be, it was intended as a status symbol of a kind, a demonstration of a gently reared woman's refinement and accomplishment, and so it belongs to a different tradition. It was made to indicate, in part, that its maker had the leisure to work at it; to suggest, even, that she was not obliged to do really onerous housework.

I've wanted to preserve, through humbler objects, the lives of the more ordinary people history traditionally overlooks, and to me, these objects radiate an attitude to the world that is uplifting and positive. Their makers didn't give up, even if the world gave up on them; they may not have been sophisticated, but they were infinitely resourceful and creative, and they had a sense of fun. These objects call into question the very idea that real creativity is elitist, and that it has to take itself seriously to be serious.

To fully appreciate textile crafts you have to be able to take yourself back, in your imagination, to the time when they were made, and my touchstone for this has to be my own past. It's not that the women I knew when I was young had glamorous lives; they were small-town and rural people with low incomes and their share of misfortune, and their choices were limited by both lack of education and money. It's their sheer ordinariness, however, that makes them relevant. They lived as many thousands of other women did.

People still called England 'home' when I was young, including my grandmother — born here in 1901. It was as if they believed they were only here on a visit, that this New Zealand world was less convincing than distant places where they felt they truly belonged. That could be confusing to a child; I never understood why my children's books were filled with pictures of thatched cottages, squirrels and badgers. Looking out at the real world I lived in, it seemed strange because it was so un-English. Where were the robins, and why wasn't there snow at Christmas?

Like everyone we knew, my immediate family's ideas about the world hinged on the British Empire, Christianity, royalty and each other. Few of them travelled abroad, even as far as Australia, and they did not read demanding literature or expose themselves to challenging ideas if they could help it. My grandfathers and my father all fought in overseas wars, and that was a form of overseas travel, it's true; but it was not associated with pleasure. My father only went abroad again at the very end of his life, and that was to visit the scenes of the great World War II battles in the Pacific. That hardly suggests he associated travel with recreation. My grandfathers never went abroad again after they returned from World War I.

My Aunt Barbara, my mother's sister, trained as a nurse and worked overseas in the '50s. For many years she was the only woman in the family to venture as far as Europe, and the only one to have a professional qualification. She was also unmarried, and therefore free to have such adventures. Everyone else in the family I knew barely ever had a holiday, and they seldom travelled anywhere within New Zealand either. My Auntie Mary famously used to ask why you'd bother to leave the Wairarapa.

It's hard to imagine now what life was like for those women. They were nearly all financially dependent on men, fathers or husbands, and many of those men were difficult people who'd survived war, sometimes more than once. Women's magazines of the 1940s dealt with the idea of the young widow in fiction, and in their advice pages; many women during this period were widowed either by World War I or II, and many would live on widows' pensions for the rest of their lives. They accepted as inevitable what we would call hardships.

Their magazines stressed the importance of a cheerful and pretty home, of brittle feminine cheerfulness in the face of death and sickness, of the obligation to be a competent mother. Survival was the first priority, and by today's standards, ordinary people were probably unreflective.

Robin redbreasts and Christmas holly — neither of them known in New Zealand — adorn this teacloth (detail), probably 1940s.

LEFT: **I know that my Aunt Barbara knitted and embroidered this jumper during World War II because when she died I found the pattern among her things, torn from the English *Woman's Weekly* (above) and dated 10 June 1944. My aunt embroidered lazy daisies, not the stylised flowers the pattern called for. There are several wartime snapshots of her wearing it, including the one on the far right, and I wore it myself during the '70s when this style of knitwear became fashionable again.**

Although that way of life was idealised in popular song and films, it could be stifling. People were harshly judged by their families and neighbours if they stepped out of line — broke the law, perhaps, left a marriage, had an illegitimate child. There were stricter social hierarchies than there are today, when higher education, with its potential for class mobility, has become available to more people; social contact outside the family was comparatively limited. There was a degree of formality even between good friends; my grandmother's best friend lived further along the same street all their married lives, but they never addressed each other by their Christian names, and never visited each other on impulse. Most small-town people had little contact with people from other cultures. Chinese greengrocers were the sole exception in my world.

Love that endures must be active, creative and purposeful.

QUOTATION MY MOTHER WROTE INTO THE BACK OF A RECIPE BOOK WHEN SHE WAS FIRST MARRIED.

I can't say that all the marriages I knew of were happy, or that my family talked of marriages they knew of in the past in those terms, either, but people stayed together out of a sense of duty, if they possibly could, especially if they had children; divorce was scandalous and unusual.

It could be a sad marriage where a woman sat and stitched an imaginary world, and where she dreamed of other choices she could have made. Many women must have ultimately found the optimism expressed in their embroidered trousseau items ironic. An embroidered apron from the 1930s in Te Papa's collection has a note attached from its maker, labelling her project 'misapplied enthusiasm'.

My two grandmothers, born at the end of the 19th century, and the beginning of the 20th, lived very different lives.

Rory, my father's mother, came from a middle-class Methodist home in Auckland; her family had been missionaries. She married just as my grandfather Douglas went away to war. He came back to farm the land his father had set aside for him, but he was never, at heart, a farmer. Rory became an invalid, a decision I suspect was strategic; my grandfather was domineering, and she had no other way of expressing independence or rebellion. As far as I know, she did not do handwork.

My other grandmother, Lucy, grew up on a small Wairarapa farm at Whareama, the second of nine children. Her mother Alice had been a servant, born on Banks Peninsula, who met her husband when he worked as a ploughman on the same Wairarapa sheep station. Later on, she became the postmistress at Tinui. Alice also ran the family farm; her husband was a good deal older than she was, and died while she still had young children to look after.

Lucy left school at 14 to go to work as a servant for a Masterton family. She'd made plans to train as a Karitane nurse by the time she met my grandfather, Billy Allan, but those plans were abandoned when they settled down to run their little market garden on the outskirts of town.

The house where Lucy lived was built in the 1920s, about the time she married. But she and Billy did not have the pleasure of living in their new house for long; during the Depression she and my grandfather had to rent it to tenants who could afford to live in it, in order to pay the mortgage.

My mother and sister were raised, then, in a two-roomed bach on the property, which I later lived in, in turn, with my mother. In between times, my now-widowed grandmother rented it out to people building homes in the streets nearby. It had been built by my grandfather for that purpose when he planned the house.

Once she was living in her own house, my grandmother took in foster children, and found other ways to generate a little income.

She sold walnuts from her two trees to local greengrocers, and took in boarders who lived in what would have been her sitting room; she and everyone else lived in the kitchen. With that money, and her pension, she managed. She grew her own fruit and vegetables, as she had always done, and had hens. It makes sense to me that with that virtual peasant subsistence lifestyle, so like that of her ancestors in England and Germany, she also made textile handcrafts. There was no self-consciousness about it; it was necessary, but it was also a pleasure.

I also think she had something to prove; she had lost the sight of one eye, but her handwork was exact and careful; you would never have been able to tell, looking at what she made, that she had a disability.

When I grew up, in the 1950s, there was one outside toilet for our household, across the back porch, but in her day this luxury meant my grandmother had fancier plumbing than any of her sisters, who lived on outlying farms. Lucy still cooked on a coal range, like most New Zealanders at that time, and did her washing once a week in a copper. Until my uncle married in 1960, and came to live there with his new wife, the house had no modern facilities of any kind, other than electricity. The hot water came from a cylinder heated at the back of the coal range, and we bathed once a week, as most people we knew did, in shallow warm water that we often had to use after another family member. The house was unlined, other than with scrim and wallpaper, and uncarpeted. It was cold in winter, but only one room was ever heated, by the coal range, because of the cost of electricity. If we wanted to use a telephone, we arranged that ahead of time with neighbours across the road. This lifestyle was not unusual, then, and my grandmother was not sorry for herself.

Woollen fabric needle holder with felt flowers, 1930s–40s.

My grandparents had lived in near poverty on this three-quarters of an acre during the Depression, a time Lucy called 'The Slump', but seldom talked about. They grew their berries and sold them in season, and they had a cow which they kept in a paddock across the road. Milk from the cow enabled them to just get by. My mother and her sister never recovered emotionally from the cruel taunts of fellow schoolchildren whose parents were better off, and like many people who had similar experiences, they wanted desperately to put that humiliation behind them when they grew up.

Of course Lucy made all their clothing; her parents gave each daughter a sewing machine when they married, and she had little choice anyway. My mother and Barbara had pet angora rabbits, and one luxury in their life was the jumpers Lucy knitted from their clipped wool. That memory, perhaps, came to my mother's mind when she embroidered the fluffy tail onto my dressing-gown rabbit.

My mother, Joyce, was 13 when World War II began. She and her family continued to live from hand to mouth during those years as they had done in the Depression, her mother taking in washing from the American soldiers in camp nearby for extra income. Until she died, in 1972, tears would come to my mother's and my aunt's eyes when they remembered watching the young American marines march out of their camp at the Solway Show-grounds, across the road from their home, knowing many were likely to be killed in battle before long. I have her autograph album of those soldiers' signatures and messages; small-town boys, most of them, from places like Alabama and Kentucky. One of them, an especially God-fearing Christian from Los Angeles, became my godfather.

My grandmother never knew either luxury or prosperity. The only luxury my mother would ever know was the wartime money my father had saved, and lavished on her in their short marriage. Her father died, after a long illness, when the war ended.

A new dress was a big event in my family's lives, and was probably homemade from a Simplicity pattern. A new piece of furniture was expected to last a lifetime. We'd carry our suitcases from the railway station for a mile, climbing fences and walking though the nearby Masterton Showgrounds to my grandmother's house when we caught the train home from Wellington, rather than pay for a taxi we couldn't afford. Nothing that could potentially be recycled was ever discarded or wasted, and still we never got ahead. Throughout those years the women in my family stitched and knitted, made whimsical toys and presents, and created what they could that was pretty and practical to decorate their homes.

My parents' marriage broke up when I was born, and my mother's creativity and imagination went, more than ever after that, into making things from the materials she had at hand, like her mother and grandmother before her. She never stopped. If paid work as a housekeeper, shop assistant or low-ranked office worker was to offer her little sense of achievement, my mother could make her own mental challenges out of scraps of fabric, a few buttons, a scrap of lace. She could make something out of nothing — the rag doll she made from one of my aunt's white nursing stockings one afternoon, and which I carried in my pocket; the appliqué laundry bag I took away to boarding school; fringed placemats made from curtain remnants that suggested the possibility of sophisticated formal dinner parties she'd never have.

She could be a perfect wife, lacking only a husband. She could be more ingenious, more inventive than women whose lives had worked out more smoothly. By her standards, she did it right, better than the wealthier women she sometimes worked for. But she was a divorcee, and so destined to live on the margins of polite New Zealand society.

Aprons and workbags are the cornerstone of what I've collected, just as they were the cornerstones of women's domestic lives. Women were using one or other at all times at home, whether they were actively working at household chores, or creating their handwork projects in quieter moments.

Women wore aprons every day, and some must have had a small wardrobe of them. They had to protect their clothing as best they could, both from dirt and wear, because finding the money to replace them was always an issue, and laundering without machines and driers was hard work. But they made a virtue of their aprons by turning them, often, into attractive dress-up garments that made them look cheerful as they went about their work. Magazine imagery of the time has housewives posing in their pinnies as if they are high fashion, and as if they're having lots of fun flirtatiously pushing that brand-new vacuum cleaner across the carpet. Aprons even featured in erotic cartoons; I suppose because they were associated solely with captive femininity.

Magazines in the 1950s encouraged women to make mother-and-daughter matching dresses; a copy of Weldon's *Ladies' Journal* for June 1949 promotes a typical example, and my mother made patchwork aprons for herself and me with that popular theme in mind. At the centre of her apron is a piece of the hunting-theme curtain fabric she made curtains from in about 1956; the frill is made from cotton scraps from one of my school frocks. The black, yellow and grey prints are typical of my grandmother's taste. Two almost identical fabric squares in different colour ways — with a blue and a green background — were from dresses my mother and her sister had; though they were deeply competitive, they often also chose identical fabrics and china. These, and the other cheerful prints my mother used, are examples of old dress fabrics hoarded by my family since wartime. My apron has a long neck loop; it was made to be extended as I grew, so that the apron would have plenty of use. Typically of my mother, she used small-patterned pieces for this child's garment, and chose them to tone softly with each other. I recognise a doll's dress fabric, and the fabric from a baby's bib I once wore. The patches on her apron are edged with traditional multicoloured herringbone stitch.

Women had a variety of types of aprons made for different purposes — from sacking aprons for heavy outdoor work to delicate lacy aprons to play hostess in. Workbags, too, were made in an infinite variety of styles, some obviously intended for public display, and some not. My mother's hung on the corner of a chair, ready to be picked up in an idle moment, and she always wore an apron, made from the most interesting remnant she could find in fabric shops' sale bins, even after she left small-town life behind and came to the city. She made an effort to make her aprons look like fashion accessories — without ironic intention — but she would never have chosen to be photographed wearing one; they belonged to her truly private life.

A small lidded jar was recycled in the 1930s–40s by covering its lid with felt flowers, and became a dressing-table ornament.

two

Part Two: Wishing and hoping

Miniature man and woman in period costume, made from wool scraps and felt in the 1930s (actual size). Possibly intended as a novelty brooch.

Sadie got three pounds a week, with deductions. She didn't expect she would ever get any more. She didn't imagine she would rise to anything better. She expected she would marry Jack Wynne, who was a motor salesman and made a fiver a week and had hopes. Sadie supposed she loved Jack. She loved the way his hand held hers, and his kisses. She yearned for a home of her own, for a teeny-weeny flat, and being Mrs Jack Wynne.

'CRUISE' BY URSULA BLOOM, NEW ZEALAND WOMAN'S WEEKLY, 16 JULY 1936

One day my prince will come, I hope

The short story quoted on the opposite page was published on my mother's 10th birthday. On the outskirts of Masterton, on a block of land that grew just enough vegetables to help them get by, and with a cow grazing over the road for their milk, her family was just managing to hold itself together. At Masterton West School, the rich children taunted the poor, in the depths of the Depression, in a way she would never forget, and the economies practised by her mother would become the habits of her own lifetime.

My mother was living in the small, two-roomed bach on the property with her parents and her sister when she was 10 years old. Her parents didn't get on, that must have been all too apparent, but for the remaining 37 years of her life, my mother would never give up her dream that one day her prince would come, that a dream marriage was really possible, that Snow White (herself) would wake to the kiss of a handsome provider, like she did in the animated film by Walt Disney. For that matter, my grandmother, in all other ways a practical woman, never stopped reading romantic fiction until the day she died. Maybe by then it had become complete fantasy for her, a relaxing escape into an imaginary world of total unreality. But it never became that for my mother, a child of the '30s. Maybe the movies, which had brought romantic fiction so vividly to life for her generation, were partly to blame.

Like Sadie in the *Women's Weekly* story, like most New Zealand women, my mother would never earn much money. She went away to art school in Dunedin after she left school, intending to become an art teacher, but shocked the maiden aunts she boarded with by showing far too much interest in men, and was soon packed up and sent home again. She was pretty and flirtatious, rebellious, and cooped up in a small town when she met my father and thought she saw her way out. She thought he was like the character of Ashley in *Gone With the Wind*, who she preferred to the more virile Rhett Butler. He was the sensitive type, I think she meant; in his soldier's portraits he looks like a war poet.

What could be more romantic than a gentle dance by the potted ferns, to the strains of a distant orchestra? This romantic couple is stitched in fine detail, and with great skill. While most women were content simply to embroider the outlines of purchased projects such as this in coloured thread, a few women spent many hours colouring them in with endless tiny stitches. The woman's dress is embroidered so carefully you can see where the creases of her garment would naturally fall, and the embroiderer has even managed to convey the outline of the man's black dinner jacket lapels, as well as the band down the side of his trouser leg, although they are all worked in black. She has also made the buttons on his waistcoat stand out. The woman's downcast eyes suggest aloof sophistication, and her partner gazes at her in calm admiration. He looks strangely Chinese. I'm in two minds about this image: partly I see it as a fantasy, escapist image of a single woman with a man as a useful prop, and partly I see it as an image of conventional courtship in an exotic locale. Then again, it might just have been a local dance studio.

Dance studios provided popular entertainment in the 1930s, and must have served as a way of getting eligible (and respectable) young men and women together. The *New Zealand Talkies and Theatre* magazine of July 1931 reported faithfully on many dances and dance schools around the country.

'Members of the Titahi Golf Club and their friends assembled in full force at the Adelphi Cabaret on the 19th June, when their annual ball was held. The weather conditions were not of the best but this did not deter the enthusiasm of the golfers, and the rain and wind outside were completely forgotten in the cosy atmosphere of the Cabaret. It was a cheerful gathering and the committee had left nothing undone to ensure a happy time. The hostesses were Mesdames S. Brice (wearing a gown of black and grey georgette), H.A. Bown [sic](red and gold), and J. Alexander (in black lace).'

Well, these were decorous times, and your frock was bound to be more important than anything you had to say.

Joyce's story, up till that point, could have been one of the romantic stories that were, at this time, avidly read by women; they always ended decorously, with a proposal of marriage. Only in her case life continued after the proposal: there was a wedding, but there wasn't a happy ending. A glory box full of embroidery was not going to be enough to carry her through, and she would pawn and redeem her diamond engagement ring regularly for the rest of her life, whenever she fell on hard times.

When I was a child, my mother would sometimes spend a quiet hour or two showing me the contents of that glory box, including the treasures she had accumulated in expectation of marriage. It contained things we never looked at otherwise: a Chinese doll with an embroidered jacket and hat; a Maori doll with a flax cape from the Centennial Exhibition in Wellington in 1940; miniature candlesticks for a dinner table that would never be set; the prize *Child's Companion and Juvenile Instructor* her father had been given at school in the 1880s, from which she would read me Wordsworth's sorrowful verses — a favourite was 'Master, We Are Seven'; and the embroidered tea cloths and tray cloths she had worked before marriage. These were lifted out, unfolded and admired. Some would never be used; others would be used and become ruined, in these days before reliable stain-removal products. There, too, were the bridal floral crepe-de-Chine nightdresses she had smocked, and which I would wear, in my teens, because I thought they were glamorous reminders of old movies.

There is every reason to believe that women continued sewing for their glory boxes during the Depression, despite their lack of ready money, as Joyce must have done during the war. The transfer-printed projects were expensive to buy, however. An unworked tablecloth I have from this era cost 27s.6d; thread would have added to that cost, and that was pretty well a week's wages for a woman. In my English Oxendale summer mail-order catalogue of 1931 you could buy a smart, casual two-piece suit with a blouse for only threepence more, but a bride's household linen was expected to last a lifetime, just as her marriage was, so quality linen was considered a worthwhile investment.

A glory box was, of course, the equivalent of a bride's dower chest from the more distant past, or the filled linen cupboard a girl from a European peasant background would traditionally bring to her husband's home. In my mother's case the glory box was a modern 1940s affair with chrome handles, and a sunburst design in veneer on its lid.

I grew up reading my grandmother's romantic fiction and women's magazines along with my own children's books in the 1950s, and saw little difference between them. These soft-covered romance paperbacks formed high piles by my grandmother's bedside, and I sometimes slept in the twin bed on the other side of her bedside table. From them I learned that pretty outback nurses in Australia had first dibs on the handsome doctors of the world; that men who seemed to be arrogant and unreachable would soon be humbled by a good woman's gentle simplicity and neatly ironed floral cotton frocks; that rich young women in jodhpurs who insisted they only wanted independence, as they tapped their thighs with riding crops, would unaccountably fall for men with low incomes but noble souls, and count themselves blessed to be able to humbly darn their socks.

Reality, I came to realise at a young age, bore a baffling lack of similarity to fiction. But in women's lives at this time there was a strong desire, it seems to me, to avoid reality and concentrate on dreams. That is what their needlework suggests.

Nobody quite knew why my grandmother had married Billy Allan, for example, though she was such a devotee of romance on paper. He was nearly 20 years older than her, known to be a difficult man in the country community where she grew up, and where he was a travelling buyer of hides and skins. My grandmother's cousin Emily, when she was very old, told me facetiously that Lucy had married Billy for his section. My grandmother loved gardening, it's true, and the three-quarters of an acre he owned was a massive gardening project for her to tackle. Well if that was true, it was at least a practical basis on which to start a marriage.

I have a letter my grandfather wrote to Lucy when she was away staying with her mother during wartime not long before he died, and in its own way I recognise it as a love letter many turbulent years later; it would be why she kept it. He describes her successful onion crop, which he has harvested, and to her, his plain prose on a subject so near to her heart would have been as good as lyrical. They obviously had an understanding on one level that worked for them — but that is love of a different kind from what young women daydream about, and very different from anything you would ever have read in the *Woman's Weekly* fiction pages.

My mother, in her turn, married my father within six weeks of first selling him tobacco. Naturally she barely knew him, or he her, but he was quiet, had good manners and was nice-looking, and she must have looked a lot like the mysterious Italian girls whose photographs, inscribed 'To Mackie', he'd brought back from the war.

Romantic fiction, published in cheap paperbacks, was popular in the 1950s. It was my grandmother's usual bedtime reading.

Also it was 1947, he bought her a band of five diamonds, and people were marrying all around her; it was the thing to do. The highest ever number of marriages celebrated until that time in this country, 20,535, was recorded in 1946. The years between 1943 and 1947 were also record years for divorce, but I doubt whether anyone was thinking about that when my mother walked up the aisle in white, her sister and sister-in-law following sour-faced in hideous teal bridesmaids' frocks, and beamed her triumph at the photographer.

My mother was a believer in marriage, as her mother had been before her, in spite of having her dream fail soon enough after that ill-fated wedding. She believed that somewhere there was another man who would fall in love with her, marry her and pay her bills for ever after. The idea that she would support herself, or have a career, was quite alien to her; we knew hardly any women who lived like that; to lack a husband then was a far greater failure than lacking an education.

The movies of her childhood and young adulthood, and romantic fiction, may have had a lot to answer for, but so did the times my mother lived in. It was not possible to live with a man without marrying him; it was not possible to have an active sex life while unmarried without risking social ostracism and pregnancy; it was barely possible to have a social life, once you were in your 20s, without a husband to accompany you; and after you were 30 you were considered to be unmarriageable.

In 1951, by which time she was a solo mother, the vast majority of New Zealand women over the age of 16 were indeed married, 431,176 of them. Although 153,199 had never married, most of them were under the age of 24; they surely would marry in time. Nearly 16,000 women were divorced or separated, but they were such a small minority they barely rated comment.

Most women's ideas of courtship and marriage were surely formed by the movies, at this time, as well as by the romantic fiction they read avidly, and a good deal of this seems to have been costume drama. The images of courtship women embroidered harked back to an Arcadian fantasy of the 18th century, a costume-drama past of men who bowed low to ringletted women hands in gallant tribute to their beauty.

When 'E' (whose initial is embroidered but not visible here) embroidered this apron in the 1930s she must have been under the influence of costume dramas in the movies, as well as popular romantic fiction set in the past. The courting couple is dressed in a style reminiscent of the 18th century, a time which seems to have captured the collective imagination, inspiring fashion clothing as well as needlework projects and china, and which connects to the craze at this time for images of traditional English cottages. Maybe, in part, this was about the Commonwealth countries, far apart as they were, recognising their united origins. As is usual in this kind of work, the male figure is oddly feminine. He is busy adoring the female, who gazes off into middle distance while he tries to hold her close. She surely has her heart set on the worthy goal of marriage before she submits to any further intimacies.

Embroidered pincushion, possibly Polish.

These are the daydreams of girls who imagined exotic settings, times other than this, and men who were tame. I think of them as a bit like the posters young girls like me would later pin to their bedroom walls, of girlish boys in pop groups whom we were never likely to meet. But these courtship images were made by grown women in a more ingenuous time. The movies were not yet about gritty reality and violence; they served a need for escape into comforting dreams, and women in hard times had need of dreams. Maybe these embroidered men, like our later pop stars, negotiated the gap between childhood and adulthood — especially sex — in a way that made it seem less alarming.

Women's lives were more sheltered during the '30s, '40s and '50s than they are now. They tended to live at home with their parents, as the women in my family did, or they boarded with families who expected them to behave respectably, as did my grandmother's boarder, Ngaire. Some lived in supervised hostels, like those run by the YWCA. In a society of small towns, and cities the size of large towns, women had to guard their personal reputations or lose any chance of a good marriage by getting a 'bad name'. Courtship was conducted in public, in small communities where there was little privacy and limited mobility; far fewer people had cars than do today.

Virginity was still expected for brides, and without reliable contraception many women must have been well motivated to qualify. Illegitimate children had to be given up for adoption; there was no chance of a respectable marriage otherwise, and marriage was both necessary and inevitable for women who were brought up to expect not to support themselves.

In 1931 63,107 women earned between £52 and £156 a year, while more than a quarter of a million New Zealand women had no income at all. Men earned significantly more. They also had their jobs protected. Radio's Aunt Daisy, for example, temporarily lost her job on 2YA that year because of a government instruction that only men were to be employed at the station during the Depression. She was her family's sole breadwinner at the time.

From 1947–49 there were 61,745 taxpaying women, but 399,535 taxpaying men, the discrepancy in numbers an indication of how married women were typically supported by their husbands, sole providers for their families. Women who had a personal income of more than £200 could be assessed for tax jointly with their husbands, but there were just 7,302 women in a position to do that. The incentive to marry must have been strong, for economic even more than romantic reasons.

But how to get a man to propose? How to attract him, without losing one's dignity and reputation? How to be seductive, yet respectable?

It must have been no easy thing to storm the citadel that was a woman, in these days before the pill, though obviously it could be done. There was a marked rise in illegitimate births at the end of World War II, for example. 'War influences, resulting in unusual movements of the population and the influx of servicemen to the more heavily populated centres, no doubt are responsible for the high figures recorded during 1943–46,' the official yearbook of 1947–49 deadpans.

There are no images of soldiers embroidered by women at this time, to my knowledge. In fact, the images of embroidered men in my collection date from the 1930s, when the marriage rate plummeted along with the economy, a trend that recurred during the coming war years for obvious reasons. Real men had a great many options available to them in their work or careers, but women limit them in their embroidery to roles as restricted as their own; they are just one half of a courtship.

It seems to me that a woman must have partly relied on her efforts at glamour to arm her against casual seduction. Clothing and hairstyles of these decades would have helped maintain the idea that she was not to be lightly seduced and abandoned. Women were corseted tightly from their shoulders through to their thighs, and wore layers of undergarments: bra, singlet, petticoat, corset, knickers. A corset was crucial, otherwise garments did not sit well. Women's hair was set stiffly on rollers, and hairsprayed till it was hard. It was only washed once a week, and women slept with their hair wrapped around rollers, or in hairnets which tied under their chins, to protect their coiffures. The fabrics women then wore creased easily, and many garments

Marry her and get her out of the office. She is evidently one of the women who are temperamentally unfit for business, and whose proper sphere is a home where they can be monarch of all they survey.

DOROTHY DIX, NEW ZEALAND WOMAN'S WEEKLY, 16 JULY 1936

and accessories had dye that was not colourfast; it was disastrous to be caught out in the rain, or to spill a drink. Hats had to be worn in public, and so did gloves and stockings. Faces were powdered all over, and lips were carefully painted; little was left to chance, even if 'looking natural' was considered admirable.

Strict attention to grooming is evident in the images women sewed of themselves; they seem to invite a chivalrous response, and chaste admiration. Self-control seems to be the acknowledged rule. And of course, in the movies there were only single beds. Even married couples slept in twin beds, and if they were filmed in their bedroom, according to prevailing American regulations, they had to kiss decorously with one foot on the floor.

A wedding, the pinnacle of court-ship, was known as 'Her Day'. It was the day when a woman fully entered the adult world, when she must look her best, and radiate her confidence at her choice of husband, as my optimistic young mother did. It was as costly an exercise as her family could afford, involving not only the ceremony and function afterwards, but also the wedding gown and obligatory trousseau to be worn for 'going away' after the wedding, and on her honeymoon. I suspect this was the last time many women would ever be able to lavish money on themselves, the last time many would have a decent wardrobe, and the last time many had a real holiday.

What was life going to be like for New Zealand women, once they were wooed and won? Would it meet the expectations they depicted in their sewing projects, of cosy cottages with hollyhocks at the door? Probably not.

Every morning, from the 1930s through to 1963, New Zealand women turned their radios to the famously garrulous Aunt Daisy's morning radio programmes. The theme tune for her show was 'Daisy, Daisy, give me your answer, do,' and whoever worked this apron was obviously enjoying a play on words when they embroidered those words on the pocket in the 1930s. The courtship image of the young man and woman contains very necessary elements for the time. There is a tree with a seat beneath, where a courting couple can sit — in full public view, of course. There is a bicycle built for two, as there is in the song, which indicates that the young couple can spend innocent hours together, engaged in whole-some exercise, while they get to know each other. And through the gate, by the fence with climbing roses and hollyhocks, there is a glimpse of a suitable cottage for them to live in once they've tied the knot. He wears a cravat with a wing-collared shirt; I feel sure he has a good job — as a bank teller, perhaps. She is dressed girlishly, with a hint of nostalgia for an earlier era, and carries a flower-adorned hat which would surely be suitable for wearing to church on Sundays.

My secret life

Sadly, this truly dashing figure only adorns a bag for dusters. Her look of hauteur, and her slash of bright red lipstick suggest she is independent-minded, and the suggestion of cigarette smoking — the smoke forming the lettering — evokes the way 1930s film stars used smoking as a way of indicating their sophistication. Really nice girls were less likely to smoke in the movies than girls who were independent, challenging and perhaps thought of as less delightfully feminine.

The reality of most women's lives was this man or that, sooner or later, and marriage. Only a handful could hope to have a career path and financial independence during the '30s, '40s and '50s, even if they wanted to. Children, in times of unreliable contraception, would be almost inevitable. Higher education for women was a rarity.

Possible career options, if a woman were to remain single, were mostly traditional ones; teaching and nursing featured prominently, and they are female-dominated workforces to this day. Both these traditional jobs might lead to fulfilling and independent lives, even to travel and work abroad, but neither was well paid and both meant conforming with strict social expectations of decorous behaviour.

Nurses working for hospitals lived in closely guarded hostels where they lived by strict house rules, rather as they might have in a boarding school, under the watchful eye of matron. Their independence, even though they were working adults, was constrained. Female teachers could not expect to become heads of coeducational schools, although they might well have sole charge of small country schools, and they did not enjoy equal pay.

In 1930 the pay scale for head-masters ranged from £570 to £860 a year, and for headmistresses from £430 to £670 a year. Male assistant teachers were paid from £200 to £520, and females £168 to £408. This built-in discrepancy can only have helped to discourage ambition.

Once, when a party was being arranged in my honour by the Teacher's Institute, the president asked me whom I would like to meet. 'Oh, the headmasters and headmistresses,' I replied. When it was pointed out to me that the schools were coeducational and that the head teachers were men, I said, 'Then let's have the heads and the seconds,' thinking in this way to include the women — but not a bit of it; the seconds in command were also men, and I had to go to the thirds and in fact everybody before I could satisfy my wish to include my own sex! Thus, from early years, the New Zealand child learns to accept as a matter of course the domination of man through sex alone. Women take their places on town councils, on after-care committees, on the bench, in law, they stand high in the medical profession and attain good posts and practices, but, so far, no woman has been elected to Parliament.

M. WINIFRED GUY, WOMAN'S MAGAZINE ANNUAL, 1934

Secretarial work was thought of as glamorous, and in my own family we admired women who held down office jobs doing real paperwork, rather than merely working with their hands or being shop assistants. That was the reason why my mother chose clerical work when she moved to the city in 1960, though she was not especially suited for it; her family had selected the commercial rather than the academic course for her at college, and she'd left school at the end of the fourth form.

There was an awareness that some New Zealand women might be doctors or lawyers — a woman doctor had, after all, delivered my mother in 1926 — but the level of education required for that was impossible to achieve in households where older children had to work to support the family, and would have been thought of as a bad investment anyway, in my family, since women would only marry and never work again.

Also, it was considered bad form for a woman to deprive a man of a job, since he would have dependants and she would naturally have a husband if she had children herself. The divorced or separated mother did not rate consideration.

Spinsters were neither admired nor envied, and were often the butt of humour about their supposed lack of choice in the matter. Many single women were expected to stay at home to look after elderly parents and other family members before they earned, often too late, a life of their own. But they could not count on inheriting a fair share of their parents' estates, even after such a sacrifice; sons were a higher priority than daughters.

Most women would leave school as soon as they legally could, and mark the time until marriage living at home with their parents, working at poorly paid jobs with few prospects of promotion, or helping their mothers with household chores, and expecting to end up with a life rather like their mothers' in the end.

The 1930 *Official New Zealand Yearbook* gives some comparison of girls' and boys' expectations when they left school in 1928: 137 secondary-school boys were expecting to stay at home, compared with 10 times as many secondary-school girls (1142). It was the same story with girls and boys leaving high schools, technical and day schools: 77 boys were expecting to stay home, compared with 730 girls.

Even within the workforce, it is remarkable how many women worked in jobs that directly related to the expected skills of home-makers. In 1954 one in five women worked either in education, or in hospitals and related medical work. If you combine work associated with food production, textiles, domestic and personal services with that, it was one in three working women. And if you add in the number of female retail workers to that total, it accounted for half the woman workers in New Zealand.

All those female workers were paid less than men: journeymen tailors earned £85.6d a year in 1930, but journeywomen tailors earned only £40.6d. Hotel waiters earned £78.3d; hotel waitresses just £56.3d. The situation was no different 25 years later; in 1955 journeymen tailors earned £11.9s.9d a week, while journeywomen tailoresses earned £7.4s.8d; waiters earned £8.2s.10d, but waitresses took home just £5.12s.5d.

It would be 1933 before Mrs E.R. McCombs, a widow taking over her deceased husband's seat, became the first woman member of parliament. That at least had a symbolic value for other women.

'The cynosure of every eye, she bore herself with a quiet dignity throughout what must have been for her a trying ordeal,' according to a newspaper report. 'Mrs McCombs will be the first woman with the right of entry to that Parliamentary holy of holies, the main lounge, where members in moments of leisure relax in a game of billiards.'

No wonder courtship was a subject of endless fascination in women's novels; marriage was a decision on which their whole future depended in every significant sense — social, financial, creative — and it must have seemed infinitely preferable to billiards at parliament. But in a time when marriage was expected to be forever, and divorce was rare by today's standards, it was also an abdication of the very idea of independence. There would never be a personal pay packet for most married woman again, and a married woman would never again see herself as a person in isolation from the family she dedicated her life to.

The idea of the independent career girl was becoming glamorous in 1930s movies, when a woman embroidered this decisive figure and her smart car. Women had begun driving cars in ever greater numbers since World War I; the ability to drive gave them more freedom than they'd ever had before, and the car was soon treated as a meeting place for lovers in popular fiction. The bag this woman carries could be either a small piece of overnight luggage, or a briefcase. I like to think of it as a briefcase, and of this as the only piece of embroidery I have discovered from this time that celebrates the idea of the smartly dressed working woman. She seems to have parked her own car at the kerb, and is about to walk up the path to her own front door; she surely lives daringly alone. The embroiderer has taken great care over the stitches in her suit; a front seam, even a hemline, are neatly indicated by the angle of the stitches, and the dense stitches in each section of both garments follow the natural lines they'd follow in tailored garments in real life. She wears a coloured scarf at her neck, as women often did at this time; scarves provided colour accents intended to thriftily transform one basic outfit into many different looks. She wears a smart hat with a long feather trim, and of course she also wears gloves, as any well-dressed woman going out in

public would have done at the time. She carries flowers wrapped in florist's paper — perhaps given by an admirer, but equally possibly bought by herself. Her stockings would be grey silk. The embroiderer has done especially well in delineating her clear profile with tiny stitches, and her confident gaze. She has carefully painted the woman's skin in a soft face powder shade, and used a variety of stitches to suggest an immaculate hairdo. Once again she has made her stitches flow in the direction that waved hair might. This inspirational career girl was framed and must have hung on her embroiderer's wall, a symbol perhaps of what she might have been had things turned out differently.

Women at this time had proven themselves capable of doing men's work during World War I, and they would soon do so again during World War II. But it would not be until many years later that women achieved relative equality with men in the workforce, let alone a wide choice of real professional career options.

While much textile handcraft of this time focused on the ideal of domestic nest-making, some of it featured images of what I think of as 'the me that might have been', or 'my secret life'. They may have been worked by women before they married, but they may also have been tantalising reminders to women who wished they could have had another life, one in which they were self-reliant and independent; one in which they had nobody dependent on them, and could make their own choices without deferring to a husband. Women could dream, even if real life was limited in scope.

These images of an impossibly glamorous, solitary — and childless — female figure dressed in the height of contemporary fashion must have contrasted painfully with the reality of New Zealand women's lives at a time when most taxable incomes were less than £500 a year, most working women earned much less, and the vast majority of married women earned nothing at all. These glamorous images mostly seem to date from the 1930s, and many of what I suspect are glory-box pieces of this kind survive with little evidence of use, as if they've been kept for best. How could a

It is silly to imagine that all women are pretending when they say they have no wish to marry. Simply silly. Many of them are just speaking the simple truth — and why not? We are not all made alike or cast in the same mould. For my part I hope there will always be some jolly, single women such as one I remember — the happiest and most humorous soul I ever knew. She 'liked the men', and they liked her, but marriage — no! She preferred her freedom, and kept it and enjoyed it to the end — a Victorian, too!

THE EDITOR, WOMAN'S MAGAZINE ANNUAL, 1934

woman living in the Depression afford to replace them, if they were stained or ripped? And what would justify the extravagance of putting them to use in any case?

My guess is that the aprons depicting these glamorous figures were created by as yet unmarried women imagining an alternative to their inevitable fate. The embroidery on the aprons — calling for special hand washing and delicate handling — indicates they were not intended for daily wear about the house; they were more likely to be showpieces for a hostess to impress her friends with.

Such work typically only calls for a small range of embroidery stitches; it was well within the competence of any woman with patience who chose to take it up. Women mostly used stem, chain, satin, buttonhole and bullion stitches, and they mostly worked over transfer printed images they had selected. There is scant evidence of original compositions.

The embroidered women they created invite an admiring gaze, either masculine or feminine; either masculine romantic interest or feminine envy. They are slim, not yet thickened at the waist with age or childbearing, and respectably dressed; there's no hint of coquetry. They have achieved the glamorous ideal in women's magazines and films, with immaculate hairstyles and fashionable clothes, and they radiate a glacial confidence. They pose rather as actresses did in films of the '30s, as if they are publicity stills.

Such heights of glamour would have eluded the financial reach of women who were obliged to darn the ladders in any silk stockings they were lucky enough to get; imports were drastically cut in the '30s, and the few cosmetics, perfumes and accessories that made it here must have been prohibitively expensive.

What a glamorous life these embroidered 1930s apron women lead, posing with flowers as a symbol of their own fleeting beauty. One of my favourites is the woman on this unfinished apron, who sits and dreams at her open window, in a fashionable dress. Is she dreaming of a future knight in shining armour, or has she already found him — or would she rather like to climb out that window, shimmy down the blossom tree, and run off with the handsome fellow she would have married if she hadn't listened to her mother?

But the glamorous embroidered women indicate how much women yearned for the make-believe world they found in romantic fiction, the movies and popular song. An admiring male, you feel, should enter at any moment from stage right and invite them to dance. But on the other hand, the women invariably look so self-contained and preoccupied that they might respond with a witty one-liner, and not care either way.

There must have been power and potency in the idea of being alone and glamorous, before that moment of fateful approach and the eventual yielding of your future. At this point, the figures suggest, time stands still and all options are open. The handsome prince may arrive on his white horse. The boy next door may turn into a handsome stranger who'll surprise you with his ardent, unrequited love, or a stranger in a well-cut suit may meet your eyes across a crowded room. You are in charge of what happens next, as you are never likely to be again in quite the same way. The solo women radiate a cool-headed awareness of awaiting destiny.

The 1950s found women in much the same position as they'd been during the 1930s as far as real independence was concerned; homemaking was still the expected lifestyle. Hairstyles had changed, but hair still had to be set stiffly on rollers, then matted stiff with thick hairspray to achieve the desired manicured look. Clothing had become more casual; this smart striped top would have been acceptable street wear, though it was intended as holiday wear. The embroidery (right) is one example of an original composition. It is copied from a fashion plate in *Woman and Home* magazine dated May 1958 (left). 'Brief-sleeved and brilliantly gay, it is also very versatile — you can wear it with shorts for the beach, with slacks for cycling, and with a full cotton skirt for the not-so-warm evening,' reads the jaunty copy that accompanies its knitting instructions. Modelling such smart handwork, a woman might await romantic developments with confidence.

I liken images such as this 1930s embroidered apron to the studio photographic portraits many women had taken of themselves as young single women. This was the defining time in their lives, the only time when they would truly exercise significant choice, and so they presented at their best, modelling themselves in their poses and clothing on screen actresses they had seen in magazines or fashion plates. They would seldom, after this, think their appearance was important enough to record for posterity.

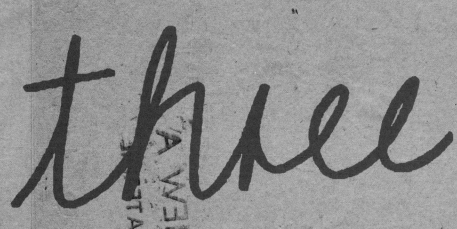

three

Part Three: Safe behind the picket fence

The cottage idyll

Miniature thatched cottage needle case, 1930s.

Simon just would not realise what modern housekeeping was like. Housewife! According to the dictionary one of the meanings of the word was 'a small receptacle holding needles and pins'. That was exactly how she felt!

'LADY IN REVOLT' BY R.A. DICK, WOMAN'S JOURNAL, SEPTEMBER 1947

When the innocent princess Snow White trilled 'Some Day My Prince Will Come' in Walt Disney's 1937 animated film, she was singing to women the world over, even in faraway small-town New Zealand, where we barely saw royalty — let alone a prince — from one decade to the next.

A girl could hope, though: my Aunt Barbara would carefully stitch Snow White onto an apron for herself in the near future; my mother, two years older, would draw Snow White Disney-style in a 1939 autograph album.

But who knew what the future held in store after Snow White leapt daintily onto the white horse with her prince, and the end credits rolled? Romance fiction never follows the newly married couple into the bedroom — it never usually gets even as far as the front door of the matrimonial home — and whatever happens next remains a mystery.

In December 1936, the year before Snow White reached cinemas, possibly the most romantic courtship gesture of the 20th century had stunned the Commonwealth. A real-life prince who'd become Edward VIII of England abdicated to marry — well, not a singing princess like Snow White, exactly — an American divorcee who looked more like her wicked stepmother. There could be no equalling that as a real love story with a grand finale, and the impact of that story could only help to confirm the centrality of love and marriage in a woman's life. She could be — as a country song later put it — Queen of the House, even if she couldn't be Queen of New Zealand. A wife was even worth giving up a throne for.

Margaret Mitchell's *Gone With the Wind* was the other great love story — fictional — of the period. Published in 1936, the year of the abdication, the novel became a motion picture in 1939, just as World War II started, starring Vivien Leigh and Clark Gable. This epic romance set in the American Civil War was the most popular movie ever, and was also, in its way, a kind of prototype of high romance, in which the crafty vixen played by Leigh lost out to the force of true traditional feminine goodness, as played by Olivia de Havilland. The period costumes — full-skirted crinolines — in that film both influenced and reflected high fashion, echoing the popular Dolly Varden (or Sunbonnet Sue) decorative theme displayed so often in '30s needlework. The real little woman as virtuous homemaker would inevitably be triumphant once

more, surely, just as she had been in a former turbulent time of war and insecurity. This was the timely message.

New Zealand women, their needlework shows, were devout believers in the cottage idyll — which was, of course, what Snow White lived with the seven dwarves after she escaped from her stepmother. They would marry and settle down in a cottage just like those in Old England, with a flower-strewn front path, orderly vegetable garden, rambling roses over the door, a dovecote perhaps. Indoors, there would be a display of immaculate housekeeping, like that of Snow White herself, who sang so prettily in the film as she swept the dwarves' floor.

The first authentic home story began in the Garden of Eden, and from then onwards all through the ages men have worked and fought for their homes, and women have made the comfort and homeyness, with the children as the crowning joy; family life being the real essence of home life — just simple, happy, loving family life! We remember — indeed we never can forget — the glorious heroism and high courage with which our gallant men went away to the Great War and fought to keep our homes safe. Fought and died by thousands, while thousands more fought and suffered, but did not die. These came back to us — broken, maimed, blind or with shattered nerves — having given all that men prize, all that makes life worth living.

NURSE SPICER, WOMAN'S MAGAZINE
ANNUAL, 1933

What could be more romantic? What better role could a woman play? And just think: marriage would last even longer in New Zealand than anywhere else, the official yearbook of 1931 tells us; life expectancy for men was an impressive 65, and 67 for women, the longest known in any country at the time.

An English cottage represented a great deal; it was a symbol of the Englishness that had survived — and been the victor — in two world wars by the time the 1950s ended. The Festival of Britain was a celebration of national pride in 1951, and the Queen's coronation two years later, with its display of pageantry, kept that pride alive.

All of this was relevant to us in New Zealand because the vast majority of us had family ties to England, and even as the British celebrated their own history and pageantry, we had our own related celebrations. The centennial in 1940 marked a hundred years since the Treaty of Waitangi, and the provinces were facing their own individual centennials as well.

We may look back now on the idea of marriage in the '30s, '40s and '50s and see it as a life sentence for women who would have to sublimate their intelligence and deny themselves, as individuals, all aspiration and self-expression. That is a modern reading of it, but these were not fully modern women; they did not yet have the ability to make choices, because they could not reliably control their reproductive lives. Without that control, and if they chose to marry, as most did, they could not rely on forging a career path on their own account. They had to buy into the fantasy of happy, singing domesticity to some degree if they were to be content with their lot, to see the cottage idyll as a kind of profession in itself.

Maybe marriage was less of a compromise than we think, more a role in which women took centre stage in their own minds, and maybe that sense of importance was not entirely imaginary. They would have control of a household, where the workplace denied them equal pay and opportunity, or the opportunity to advance to senior positions of responsibility. They would be in charge of raising a family, still thought of universally as vital work.

I doubt that most thought the day-to-day problem-solving of domestic life, and the practice of textile crafts and other domestic arts, were trivial. Women's magazines celebrated their role, and they were encouraged by them, as well as society at large, to take pride in how well they performed the role of housewife and mother.

What's more, there was a degree of independence in their life; in the hours when their husbands were at work (or overseas at war) women were accountable only to themselves. As well as that, their magazines encouraged them to develop a kind of moral authority; religion was still a force in peoples' lives, and they were in charge of inculcating those values in their children. If marriage was the cornerstone of a stable society, they were in charge of making it work. They were to be a bulwark of conservative values in troubled times, of continuity in times of threatened change.

Tea-cosy cover (above) and duster holder embroidered in cottage themes, 1930s–50s.

**Sacking-backed oven cloth showing
a cottage theme, cut from a piece of
curtain fabric, with patchwork
edgings, 1950s.**

Never mind the drudgery; though the cottage idyll lacked dish-washers, wall-to-wall carpet, electric stoves, vacuum cleaners, central heating, washing machines and clothes driers, or even an inside toilet, women were exhorted to look beyond that to the big picture. They were part of a country and a Commonwealth beyond that, and they were pre-dominantly Church of England. The merger of God and England was automatic, and you couldn't look higher than that.

Probably the ideal of the cottage idyll dates back even before Romanticism in the 19th century led to William Wordsworth's popular poems about cottage dwellers and the truth and simp-licity of their lives. My mother learned those poems at school in the '30s, and read them to me when I was a child.

The imagery of the cottage idyll, as handcraft tradition would consciously develop it here, may originate a century earlier, when the influential French philosopher Jean Jacques Rousseau developed the idea of the 'natural' man, a person in touch with nature, lacking in sophistication in the worldly sense and all the better for it. That idea was slowly developed and popularised in literature, poetry — like Wordsworth's — and art in the 19th century; as Europe became increasingly industrialised, the past seemed increasingly idyllic. Simple cottage people led lives of simple goodness, went the message; there was probably more true virtue in humble cottages than in palaces. Anglicans must have approvingly thundered out 'Jerusalem' at church during these three decades, as we did in the '50s at my boarding school, endorsing William Blake's visionary verses of protest against industrialisation:

And was Jerusalem builded here
Among these dark, Satanic mills?

We could sing about England without self-consciousness or irony because it was somehow our true home still, and you can understand the appeal of the poet's message when towns and cities were fast sprawling across the English countryside, their factories belching smoke into the air and toxins into waterways. In hard times like the Depression it must have been comforting to look back as the poet did to when our ancestors, far from here, were still self-sufficient, practising traditional crafts, and living off the produce they grew in their own small holdings. Images of deeply gabled cottages with colourful, crowded gardens dominated book illustration, calendars, embroidery patterns and household china; even contemporary architecture of larger houses carried that theme through on a grander scale in the '30s.

The cottage idyll was a retreat into collective nostalgia that people seem to have shared the English-speaking world over as reality became increasingly hard to bear. Beyond the cottage was a possibly fearful world. Even Snow White had the dark and threatening forest in which a woodcutter was expected to kill her, and through which her wicked stepmother would come to poison her when he failed in his mission. War loomed, then became reality. But within the cottage's four walls all was eternally safe and predictable.

Outside the wind has cried itself to sleep. The brief winter twilight is fading into night and in the deepening dusk the lighted lamps bloom like giant jonquils. In the silence and the safety of this firelit room there's a memory and a promise for those thousands far away. This friendly hearth, this shining room remind us that while men make houses women make homes. In the quiet welcome of this peaceful room how easy to forget you're in a house, and only know that you're at home. And how much this happy room owes to little things: to a little care with gentle Silvo; to linens made lustrous white by that last rinse in Reckitts Blue; to Zebo's winning way with gloomy grates; and to copper and brass all laughing and gay because of Brasso.

ADVERTISING COPY, BRITANNIA AND EVE, MARCH 1945

Making a home remains the greatest of all adventures. And running a happy and successful home is more than ever now, for a woman, the greatest possible test of character and intelligence, good humour and good faith.

THE BOOK OF GOOD HOUSEKEEPING, 1948

RIGHT: **This 1940s–50s knitted thatched cottage tea cosy sits on its own separate padded base for extra insulation.**

The cottage idyll was still genuinely possible for ordinary people in New Zealand, what's more, where industrialisation had not had a chance to consume the bush and the countryside, and we did indeed build simple cottages — on quarter-acre sections. But ours did not resemble the traditional English ones; thatched roofs were not suited to this climate; bricks couldn't withstand earthquakes; we built in wood, as they did in Australia and America. Yet the wooden cottages we built did not feature in any of our needlework, although we saw nothing else around us, and women seem to have had no problem accepting that.

At my father's farm the original homestead had followed the usual mid-19th-century colonial pattern; one small, basic room became a two-roomed cottage; two rooms became three; those first rooms became out-houses to a bigger, two-storied cottage built from wood milled on the property, its upstairs bedrooms reached only by a ladder, as had been the case in old English cottages too. A new homestead was then built nearer the road; the possums and birds slowly took over the first; and in my family an abandoned pioneer home like this was often called an 'old whare'.

Old whares were still dotted everywhere around the Wairarapa in my childhood; this is one of few examples of my family adopting a Maori word as being the most useful, but the term was never used by them for a cottage that was still lived in.

The first McLeod cottage had been fancifully called 'Rosebank'; perhaps my great-great-grandfather had intended climbing roses to tumble over the door as they would in later embroidery patterns; but even the roses were long vanquished by scrub and regenerating bush by the time I was a child.

Carriage tracks from long ago could still be traced in the grass, and there was a strong sense of remoteness from the world there even in the late 20th century. An uncle who'd suffered a serious head injury while felling trees, according to my family, had wandered those hills playing the bagpipes a hundred years earlier. Wordsworth would have been in Romantic raptures at the quaint simplicity of it all. My great-great-grandmother died there with her children around her, while her husband rode off in vain for a doctor. That was more like pioneer reality.

The cottage idyll in 19th-century New Zealand had, of course, no handy village to sustain it, but in the 1930s the population of the Masterton borough, where my mother's family lived, was less than 9000. To my grandmother, many of these people were as well known as her own large family; she knew their histories and intermarriages.

My mother, living in her mother's bach when her marriage disintegrated, saw that humble building as part of the cottage idyll she would like to live, or at the very least as having the potential for a housewifely role-play. She drew an idealised pencil sketch of it in 1959 that shows she was a believer still; there's a climbing rose over the door — I don't remember it, though it was there in photographs — and a cat curled up asleep outside.

In the 1940s, as a very young woman, she had clipped pictures from magazines of the effect she wanted to create inside her future home. They are in the English cottage tradition, too: a hearth, a fire, upholstered armchairs, a mantelpiece with china on it, fresh flowers in a vase, and perhaps an embroidered tea cloth laid on a table with tea things spread out neatly on it. Outside the window I suppose there should have been the English Lake District; instead there was my grandmother's bungalow, a row of standard roses under the washhouse window with a border of chives beneath them, and a wilderness on either side of her cultivated garden of lichened fruit trees and long grass.

Inside my grandmother's house, too, the cottage tradition held sway. The placement of objects around the coal range she cooked on, the old pendulum clock and Toby jug on the mantelpiece above it, the gate-leg table, the pot plants flowering on a deep window ledge — all paid unconscious tribute to traditional cottage kitchen layouts in England, where her ploughman father, the most recent immigrant in my personal family tree, had been born in 1860s Oxfordshire.

Where was the man in my mother and grandmother's cottage idyll? There was none now, other than visitors; my uncle was only 10 years older than me, and didn't qualify yet. The most confident depictions of suitable husbands in the '50s, and the two decades before them, were in the knitting patterns which I call, collectively, 'Knit Me a Husband'. These led on, in their turn, to 'Knit Me a Baby', and 'Knit Me the Children'. Magazines for women were full of knitting patterns; they must have been a strong selling point.

Even those knitting patterns evoked the long-standing cottage-dweller's custom of dressing your family through the skill of your own hands; knitting is only a few steps away from weaving, and a century before, ploughmen like my grandmother's father had worn homespun linen smocks, hand-embroidered with imagery drawn from their trades, and styled in the tradition of their region. A few agricultural workers still wore these smocks in 1930s England, where cottage life continued at that time, for some, almost unchanged since a century earlier.

The ideal husband of my mother's knitting pattern era wore elaborately home-knitted multicoloured Fair Isle jumpers and hair oil; he often held a pipe, and he gazed into middle distance with a resolute chin. He would of course let women dress him, and he might sail model boats on a pond with a son in matching V-neck. He was a real mother's boy, in other words; he was the controllable type. My mother still knitted cable-patterned sleeveless grey pullovers for my father, but that would stop when she moved to the city and gave up believing he'd come back.

Love-story illustrations in the magazines New Zealand women read, in these three decades, featured men like those models in knitting patterns, handsome in a slightly mother's-boy way, and reassuringly unaggressive. Young boys and girls, lacking television, still read fairy stories modelled on handsome princes and their beautiful princesses, whose hands were won after fearful obstacles were overcome. The illustrations of ideal male figures in these were not, in essence, much different.

Those fairy stories may have been good training: the pattern of eventual triumph over adversity would echo real life for many. My mother's generation would have to overcome the impact of the Depression and World War II before their personal prince could win their hand, and the lucky ones would ride off together to a new state house — as close as many would get to the English rustic cottage of their dreams — twinkling on the horizon.

In the best cottage tradition the first state houses, built in Wellington in the '30s, echo the English prototype in appearance; they invite hollyhocks by the door. They were even — in a burst of idealised town planning — opposite Miramar's equivalent of an English village green.

What are the qualities the saints possess? 'Faithfulness, loyalty, courage, unselfishness, love and holiness,' says the vicar's wife, and adds that we wives practise these particular qualities as we go about our daily round, cooking, shopping, mothering, pram-pushing and mending.

THE EDITRESS' PERSONAL PAGE, *WIFE AND HOME, THE MARRIED WOMAN'S MAGAZINE*, SEPTEMBER 1950

Meanwhile women embroidered cottage imagery over all kinds of textile handwork. They made tea cosies, in infinite variety, in the olde-worlde cottage shape, detailed with English cottage-garden flowers, and they embroidered picket fences, gates and flowers as motifs on doilies, hand towels, dressing-table sets and tea cloths. The ideal home was obviously not of this place; the houses they lived in did not resemble these; and it was not of this time. In a perfect world, these pieces of handwork suggest, New Zealand women would be living 12,000 miles from here. Meanwhile, they were trying to make the model fit in a country where it had no context. Maybe they were just plain homesick.

The reality of the cottage idyll was, of course, nothing like Disney's representation of it in *Snow White*. Times were truly tough for love and marriage when the Depression bit at the start of the '30s, and would be for years to come.

Men had returned after World War I to face rocky times in the '20s, but in the '30s they would face economic hardship that would have an even more drastic impact. This went beyond mere lack of money. It affected peoples' lives — and deaths — at the most intimate level.

People did not marry in the '30s without the certainty of being able to support themselves financially — there was no welfare state yet — and with so many men out of work, they could not prom-ise the single-income stability needed to rear children. A woman's prince might come eventually, but she would have to wait. The average age at marriage of both men and women went up as a result.

Statistics from New Zealand yearbooks give some clues as to what life was like in these three decades, and implications for the imagery in women's handwork.

In 1926 just 3397 men had been 'assisted' to employment by the Labour Department: five years later that number rocketed to 30,223, and it would rise dramatically again. In 1930–31, following the Wall Street crash of 1929, and

when the population of this country was just 1.5 million, 290,000 women reported they had earned no income at all, as did 26,649 men.

Wages were about to decline; in 1936 the average male wage was £3.15s.5d and the average female wage was just £1.12s.1d — six shillings a week less than it had been a decade earlier.

Women did not feature in unemployment statistics or the 'work for the dole' scheme that was then the only form of state-funded relief for the unemployed. They barely feature in employment figures either, in these decades. Nothing is known, from such statistics, of their hardship during the '30s, but it must have been impossible to save money as a dowry in anticipation of marriage, and many newly married women must have struggled to meet their own modest needs on their husbands' dwindling — or vanishing — incomes let alone their children's. It's no wonder they made what they could for themselves — their own curtains, bed coverings, clothing, household

linen — and improvised them out of whatever fabric they had to hand. Pensions, which were already small enough, were cut, and so were wages; public servants who were lucky enough to keep full-time jobs had to accept a 10 per cent pay cut until the economy recovered. There was just no spare money.

The impact on ordinary people must have been severe. Our export market, heavily reliant on Britain, collapsed in 1930, and would fall by 43 per cent in just three years. Bankruptcies were at a record level in 1931.

In 1931 and '32 there were fewer than 10,000 weddings; there would be almost twice as many in 1939 when economic confidence had returned.

In 1931, as one indicator of the stress women were under, 30 women killed themselves. A year later 46 women died by their own hand, a phenomenal rise in statistical terms, and far higher than the male rate of increase.

Thatched-cottage tea-cosy covers, 1930s–50s.

Miss 1942

Miss Nineteen Hundred and Forty-Two,
I bare my head and pay homage to you.
Square-shouldered and jaunty, hatless and gay,
With brave self-reliance you pass on your way.

With capable hands efficient and true,
Doing the jobs that men usually do;
Doing strange work with a confident mien,
Doing your bit with your heart, mind and brain.

In trim uniform of brown, fawn or blue,
Each one determined to see this thing through;
Arduous duties so ready to take,
Great sacrifices so willing to make.

I'm nearing the end of the long, long trail,
My steps are lagging, my hands are frail;
I salute the courageous spirit anew
Found in the girls of nineteen forty-two!

GRANDPA, NEW ZEALAND FREELANCE, 23 SEPTEMBER 1942

But by 1937, while New Zealand women hummed along to 'My Prince Will Come' at the movies, weddings were back in style as unemployment slowly fell, unemployed builders got back to work building new homes, and the number of first births in 1936 to 1937 surged ahead; 44.5 per cent of all first births were within the first year of marriage in 1937. However female suicide did not slacken; 58 women killed themselves here in the year of Snow White, for reasons we can only guess at.

Very significantly, for women who were destined to produce textile handwork, the number of imported sewing machines now rose dramatically. The value of sewing-machine imports had been £99 million in 1926. In 1937 that figure rose to £262 million — and the first state houses were about to be built, where the nation's housewives would industriously use them.

In 1938 there were 15,328 new marriages, the most marriages in a year ever recorded here at the time. In 1939 the record was broken again, and there were also 570 adoptions, the second highest number on record. But the number of infant deaths was also abnormally high, as was the number of fatal road accidents now that people could afford to drive once more, as they could not during the Depression. What fortune gave with one hand, with a respite into relative prosperity, it seemed to take away with the other, and world events would burst this bubble of relative optimism.

Unfortunately for this country's women the surge of late '30s confidence — reckless or otherwise — that followed the Depression was swiftly followed by something worse. Scrimping, saving and making do returned with a vengeance, and for many women it would be as if the hard times had never gone away. Their husbands and lovers faced something even more frightening and final than anything they had just experienced; the threat of death in World War II.

There is no such thing as depressing subject matter in textile handwork in wartime New Zealand, any more than there was during the Depression. At war's end there were no tea-tray cloths featuring the battle at Monte Cassino, say, or the horrors of the Burma Road. Women's domestic textile crafts do not lend themselves to protest, social comment, or the recording of bad experiences; instead they are expected to keep the Pollyanna in women alive. The world's ills, that huge and uncontrollable aspect of life, should never be seen to cross the cottage threshold.

During these three decades women must have been struggling against the odds to maintain that position. Throughout the Depression, even in the worst of times, they had produced work whose imagery reflected only the fantasy world they wished to retreat into when times were hard — and that did not change in wartime. Brittle British-like gaiety was required of them, and keeping the home fires burning, their magazines told them so. Imagery of England was now all the more poignant because we were fighting fascism alongside Britain and the other Commonwealth countries, and overtly patriotic British themes crept into needlework. These were inseparable from our own sense of patriotism; we produced no such imagery of our own.

My mother's wartime autograph tea cloth (on page 46) is a subtle example of patriotism; it commemorates her brief army life, and I have another embroidered tea cloth commemorating the army medical corps. The images in both cloths — autographs in one; insignia, flowers and birds in the other — suggest that their real associations, with the horror of war, are being neutralised into safety by their makers. Women would have cups of tea and pass the cakes over such cloths, tactile memories of what had been a life-and-death struggle for millions of people. But that struggle had been tamed and subdued in stitches.

The New Zealand Centennial in 1940, when the first groups of men were being called up for military service, does not seem to have led to a spontaneous instant flowering of local symbolism either; a vast cache of tea cloths embroidered

Framed embroidery commemorating the 1953 royal visit (private collection).

with kowhai and pohutukawa, perhaps, or tui and bellbirds on duchesse sets. But surviving embroidery examples show a mixture of images suggesting how we saw ourselves during World War II. One framed embroidered picture, which seems to be based on a commercial pattern, features a female figure dressed in a 'Europeanised' version of Maori traditional dress, backed by an Art Deco structure suggestive of the British and New Zealand pavilions at the Centennial Exhibition in Wellington. She is framed by kiwis, ferns, sailing ships (bringing immigrants, perhaps?), English-style figures on horseback, what is probably a morepork, and yachts.

Another dated 1953–54 (left), commemorating the royal visit of the new queen, is topped by an embroidered British crown, like the one she wore at her coronation; the flowers it depicts are fuchsias — they may be intended to be native ones — a thistle flower, a rose, ferns and shamrocks. The thistle, rose and shamrocks represent England, Scotland and Northern Ireland, and the ferns New Zealand. The question of our physical distance from each other does not arise; we are mysteriously united in symbolism if not in fact.

Combined floral national symbolism like this recurs often in contemporary needlework, confirming that we did not see ourselves as a separate nation so much as one of a collection of countries given purpose by the rule of the English queen, and united in our teatime rituals.

If women were obsessed with Britain, and filling their homes with images of 'home', this wasn't grounded solely in picture-book sentimentality. Though refugees and immigrants from Europe began to trickle into the country as World War II loomed. Our poets may have been struggling in verse at this time with the idea of unique cultural identity, but to judge from women's handwork, such an idea had little interest for them. We were a little England, their handwork tells us, watching British movies, reading British magazines, fighting alongside the British — and relying on the British for most of our exports as well as imported goods.

Women embroidered Allied slogans and symbols, which must have served as hopeful messages against adversity even as they were manpowered into the war effort, and took over work that had traditionally been done by the men who were now overseas fighting. They made great inroads into the public-service clerical jobs vacated by men, and were reluctant to give them up when the men returned. But that would be part of another story.

The War Pensions Amendment Act of 1940 must have been an ominous call to reality for the dreamers of the cottage dream. It laid down maximum weekly pensions in the event of disability or death for soldiers and nurses, with grim implications for their wives and families. Ordinary people could expect only a very modest lifestyle in compensation for the death or disability of husbands and fathers taken for the war effort.

A disabled private was entitled to £2 a week, but a wife or other dependant would get only half of that. Should a private die, a widow with no children would get £1.10s a week, and a widow with a child £2. Wives of amputees could look forward to an extra £8 a year to offset extra wear and tear on their husbands' clothing.

Nurses rated bigger pensions: a disabled nurse would get £2.6d more than a disabled private each week, and a dependant other than a child half that amount. Should she die, a dependant other than a child would get £2.5s a week, but her child would get only 10s a week if she either died or became disabled. Pensions were increased in 1943.

In 1940, centennial year, 206,000 women reported they had no personal income, 103,819 women had an income of less than £50 a year, and more than half of all working women earned less than £200 a year. It was just as well they had the experience of the Depression to fall back on; they needed the skills they had learned.

At war's end, in 1945, the number of marriages was almost as great as it had been at its start, and there were 37,007 children born that year. The illegitimate birth rate and adoption rates also surged upward as people settled down once more into domesticity. In 1945, 1191 babies were adopted; in 1935, in more uncertain times, only 340 had been.

Life was not all domestic serenity in a nation of cottages, however. There were also many divorces, and there was a surge in the number of applications for restoration of conjugal rights, one way of starting a divorce process which could take years. Ten years earlier, 95 applications of that kind were made; in 1945 there were 550. The number of murders also shot up; there were four reported murders leading to an arrest or summons in 1942, but there were 27 in 1945.

Women stitched for their cottages despite an ominous hint of impending social fragmentation.

What would be the effect on women of two generations of husbands who had fought in world wars? It seems to have obliged them to keep their heads down, and perhaps to cling more than ever to the ideal in spite of reality; they would be living in a man's world for which the only known antidote was femininity. And so they stitched on.

In 1946, 47,386 men from both world wars were receiving war pensions, almost as many as had been out of work during the Depression. As well as that, 36,038 had died on active service in World War II. The intake of men into the armed forces, over the duration of the war, had equated to 67 per cent of the male population between 18 and 45. Ten thousand women, my mother briefly among them, had also served in the armed forces.

There were unpleasant side effects of wartime social disruption that women had to contend with personally. One was the 21 deaths from septic abortion in 1944, and the further 180 women who were admitted to hospital that year with septicaemia from abortions which did not kill them. It seems unlikely that women would have risked their lives to abort children conceived within marriage, and we can't know how many abortions were carried out at this time without complications, since they were illegal. The rate of gonorrhoea also shot up in 1946 with the return of our soldiers.

However, such unpleasant realities, and their implications, were not highlighted when my parents and others looked toward the future. Returned servicemen and their wives would be a conservative force to be reckoned with in this country for years to come. Wartime sweethearts' married lives would be lived — man at work, woman at home — around the model of the domestic cottage idyll for the rest of their lives. Men had earned, by defending their country at war, their authoritarian role in the family; all that was required of women was that they play their role as homemakers with conviction.

In 1947, in what was then the second-highest record year ever for marriage in New Zealand, my parents married. He is described as a sheep farmer on their wedding certificate; he actually worked

for his father, who paid him capriciously, on the family farm. She is described as the spinster daughter of an orchardist; there really was an orchard on my widowed grandmother's property, after all, even if it only amounted by now to a dozen trees at the back of her large section.

With those descriptions, it seems to me, my parents read off the page of their marriage certificate like peasants from centuries earlier in their countries of origin: Germany, England, Scotland, Ireland. I mean nothing disparaging by that; most of our ancestors were peasants at one time, after all, and my parents shared a peasant's expectation of self-sufficiency. My mother's glory box waited, full of the modern equivalent of the hand-embroidered work her female ancestors would have made, and using similar needlework techniques; he brought to the marriage his saved-up soldier's pay, and the promise of inheriting land. They would be legally married for about 15 years, but would actually live together for less than three.

The year they married was a record year for pastoral production in New Zealand, it was up 15 per cent on the year before, and nearly 70 per cent up on a decade earlier.

Women were in their rightful place; there were 337,790 taxpaying men, but just 61,745 taxpaying women. But there was an acute shortage of building materials for the many homes that needed to be built. Ominously, my parents would have to live under the same roof as my father's parents, with his adult sister, while trying to persuade my grandfather to let them move into the dilapidated original homestead cottage, Rosebank. He didn't allow it.

Between 1935 and 1949 the state built 37,000 state houses, but my parents could not move into one of those either; not while my father worked for his father out in the country. In any case, there were 52,000 people on the waiting list for them. There were government loans, 18,764 of them in 1951, under which the government lent the price of building a home to returned soldiers, with no obligation to repay while the family stayed together under one roof. Forty-nine thousand ex-servicemen had been helped into their own homes by 1955, the year I started school, but my parents had not been able to borrow that money either; my grandfather would not let them build a new house on the farm.

My mother urged my father to get a government loan for a farm of his own — 14,000 ex-servicemen were helped in that way — but my father, an only son, felt obliged to work for his parents, and also felt a romantic passion for the land which had belonged to his grand-father and great-grandfather. The clock was ticking on their marriage from the start and the land would come first, as it would in a self-respecting peasant family anywhere.

I was born three days after the defeat of the first Labour government in the 1949 election, and the rise to dominance of the farmers' party. Sid Holland was the new National Party Prime Minister, and Keith Holyoake his Minister of Agriculture and Marketing. Holland would crush the watersiders' union in the great strike of 1951; Holyoake would be prime minister in the future. Farmers in the '50s would enjoy prosperity, though my parents would not. My grandfather would proudly drive a Humber Hawk, subsidised to the hilt as his farm was by the farmers' government, but neither of my parents would ever have a driver's licence.

My parents would try living together in my grandmother's bach with the roses over the door in about 1955, but one day the Humber Hawk drew up at the front gate. My father carried his square brown suitcase down the long gravel path, wearing a pullover my mother had knitted, no doubt, and walked out of our lives.

My mother was now that very unusual person, a separated wife in the 1950s, and I became that rare and strange thing, a child of a one-parent home. My school writing exercises would feature parents who lived together, because I knew what was expected, but I have no memory of the brief cottage idyll in my grandmother's bach, when I slept in the single bed at the foot of my parents' in the small bedroom. It might as well have never happened.

My mother, in the '50s, would work as a housekeeper, and as a shop assistant. She would make herself — and me — pretty patchwork aprons. She would sew curtains for the bach windows, and paint the walls in fashionable '50s style, with a feature wall in deep red, a wall in grey, and the other walls in pale yellow. She would continue rehearsing for the ideal cottage she would never manage to own.

Being gay was her only outlet, her only way of forgetting, she who had so much to forget. 'And I must flirt with your boys,' she'd try to explain, with a moment's childlike seriousness. 'I want to love them all because they are part of you. I want them to be gay and brave with you, so that they will kill many Germans and bring you safely home again.'

STORY BY JEFFERY BLYTH, BRITANNIA AND EVE, 1942

More fortunate women played the role she wanted and they continued to practise the traditional domestic handcrafts, using them to decorate the new houses that sprang up all over the country. Though these post-war houses would be modern in style, their handcrafts would only sometimes venture into the use of fashionable contemporary fabrics or reflect current trends.

Now began, tentatively, the slow decline of the cottage idyll as people began to embrace modern decorating, the idea of the 'smart' interior rather than the cosy one, American modernism rather than English tradition. The new interiors in magazines were now uncluttered, far removed from the old cottage look. The 100,000 American troops who'd been stationed here during World War II were the biggest group of foreigners ever to arrive en masse in such a short period of time, and left a legacy in such ideas as well as illegitimate births; their interest was in newness, their confidence in their own nation-building absolute.

Maybe people just wanted to look to building the future in the '50s, too; the immediate past was hardly comforting. But women still made their own workbags and aprons, as they had always done; they were still homemakers, and they could not know that they'd be the last generation of women here to make that central to their lives.

It is difficult to precisely date textile handwork from wartime; very little of it is obviously from that era, and women did not often date their work. Clues lie in the fabrics used, and the depiction of women and children's clothing. A cloth doll with a matching bonnet and button-fronted frock (shown on page 159) is dressed in obviously 1940s style; a sugar sack apron (page 236) has pleats just like those in a tailored suit of the '40s, is a '40s skirt length, and is trimmed with patterned dress fabric that strongly evokes the period. A handmade cloth doll (page 228) with sheep's wool hair seems to be an attempt to copy a '40s commercially made doll, and the way it is dressed seems to tie it to that time, or possibly a decade earlier. Some embroidery projects closely resemble those in contemporary magazines, craft publications or embroidery patterns. The fabrics used in patchwork can be linked to identifiable dress fabric of the time, and to likely earlier materials that have been recycled with them.

What is clear is that the lifestyle of women at home remained as constant in their minds, despite disruptions and catastrophes, as their handcrafts. They were basically embroidering the same things, and crafting similar objects out of fabric, using the same methods, for 30 years — and for the same reasons.

Interestingly, both men and women are seen in this handwork only in fantasy roles; maybe women were moulding men, in these images, as they were being moulded themselves by social expectations of femininity. Maybe this was a way of holding reality at arm's length, too; the business of courtship and marriage is framed as if it is play-acting, not as if it will end in a fateful decision that a woman must stick to, whatever happens, for the rest of her life.

We can't know how women reconciled the romantic presentation of men in the movies, much like those they sewed in their courtship aprons, with the real men they wound up with. To judge from photographs of the period, New Zealand men were a rough-and-ready lot, far from elegant, and their culture was one of confident, even aggressive, masculinity. Many men of this era were, or would become, returned servicemen. They were forgiven much because of the sacrifice they'd made, but many must have been hard to live with. In 1946 19 per cent of all returned servicemen's disabilities pensions were paid for problems with their nervous system; many must have suffered from shell shock and what we would now call post-traumatic stress disorder.

The Prince Charming images that women embroidered, however, gaze at their beautiful women like the china courting figures in 18th-century costume displayed in the wealthy women's home where my mother worked as a housekeeper. Those china men were so obviously appreciative, and so gallant — in a way real husbands reeling home from six o'clock pub closing, or the RSA clubs, were unlikely to be.

Thatched-cottage tea cosy with raffia roof and Cellophane windowpanes, 1930s–50s.

The bluebirds of happiness

The bluebird of happiness — often swallow-shaped, sometimes trailing sprays of flowers in its beak — is a recurring motif in needlework of the '30s, '40s and '50s. Sometimes, too, it features with ribbon bows, symbolic of 'tying the knot' in marriage, or lover's knots.

The popular idea of the bluebird of happiness may well date back to a 1909 play of the same name by Maurice Maeterlink, in which two children search the world for happiness, only to find it in their own back yard. By the 1930s the play may have been forgotten, but its theme was surely familiar; we should be content with our lot, however humble. And so the bluebird seems to have been associated in domestic crafts with happy marriages, its presence in the home a kind of decorative talisman for the cottage idyll.

My mother embroidered bluebirds into a throw of fine cambric for covering a tea trolley; other women incorporated them into tray cloths, doilies, aprons, tea-cosy covers and much more. One of my favourite bluebird pieces is a doily featuring brightly coloured wedding bells as well, making the obvious connection; how could a marriage fail to be harmonious with that sitting on the tallboy? And what could wedding bells mean but happiness — even for the thousands of women who were to produce seven-month babies during this period, marrying in haste and perhaps about to repent at leisure?

A large doily shows a bluebird sitting amid flowers, while in an embroidered vision of the sea, a stylised sailing ship passes by. In the New Zealand context sailing ships were for a long time the only means of arriving or leaving; the boat in this setting could either suggest a safe and happy arrival, or a longing for departure, perhaps even home-sickness for a faraway country.

The popularity of sailing ships as a decorative motif in the '30s and '40s — in china and tapestry patterns in particular — may also have evoked pride in membership of the British Empire, whose power was based on supremacy at sea, and on our immigration policy which still actively favoured the British as migrants.

ABOVE: **Embroidered and painted handkerchief sachet.**

RIGHT: **Embroidery transfer motif.**

An embroidered apron features the birds bearing a garland of blossoms, and a butterfly flying beneath them; more symbolism of fleeting time and fertility; the blossom will bear fruit, just as the woman wearing the apron is expected to bear children. An embroidered tea-cosy cover features the bird flying on one side, and landed on the other. Symbolism again: the wanderer has found its home, where it sits and trills happily.

I also have an embroidered and hand-painted handkerchief sachet (left) with the bluebird depicted with a nestful of eggs; the perfect Plunket mother.

Another embroidered 1930s apron has ambiguous symbolism. A ringletted young woman in quaint period costume holds an open birdcage in one hand, while a bluebird alights on her other hand (page 108). Is she about to capture the bird, securing happiness — by imprisoning in the cage? Or is she about to set it free? Who is really the captive in this scenario, the woman who lives a constrained life, the caged bird, or both? Did some women feel their wings had been clipped when they settled down into their domestic lives, much as a caged bird's might have been? And what chance did they have of escape?

It goes without saying that there are no bluebirds in New Zealand, the flowers in these embroideries are largely imaginary, and women themselves knew their ideal world of perfect happiness did not exist in reality.

In 1951, 518,705 New Zealand women were married, legally separated, widowed or divorced (there were only 7891 divorcees). Just 153,199 women had never married, and more than half of those women were under the age of 24. The overwhelming majority of women, then, dreamed — or lived — their version of the bluebird dream. Only 16,000 had abandoned it — or found it had abandoned them.

Bluebirds for Happiness

EMBROIDERY CAPTION, *WOMAN'S JOURNAL*, DECEMBER 1939

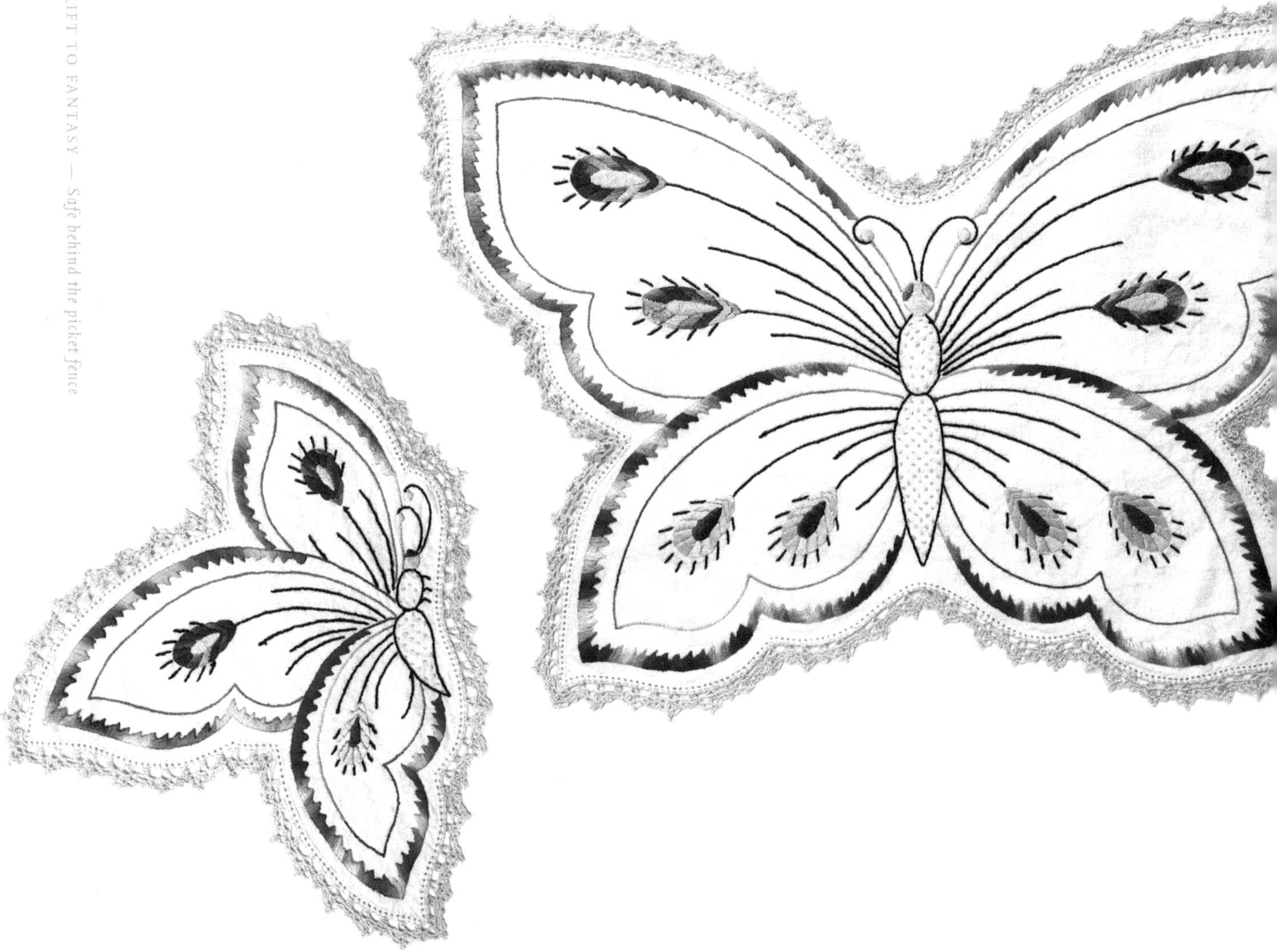

A guided tour

Our home! There is a melody in the sound of those words which is not heard in any other, whether we mean being married — our own home — or being grown-up — the home of our childhood, or — if we are just travellers up and down the highways and byways of life — then even the home of our dreams!

NURSE SPICER, WOMAN'S MAGAZINE ANNUAL, 1933

Embroidered dressing-table set with crocheted edges, probably 1930s.

THE BEDROOM

The adult bedrooms of my childhood seemed always to be chilly places with curtains drawn and holland blinds at permanent half-mast, unheated and un-carpeted, with china chamber pots discreetly concealed under the beds; many people still had unlit outdoor toilets where they would not venture at night, and the chamber pots had to be emptied discreetly in the morning. It is hard now to imagine such enforced intimacy between husbands and wives, but despite such inherent drawbacks to idealised dreams of romantic allure, within the bedroom lay much scope for needlework and textile expression.

LEFT: **A woman's bedroom at this time might feature a wide range of textile crafts, the work of herself and her family. Seen here: a 1950s patchwork dressing gown, fabric-dressed wooden doll laundry bag, embroidered and crocheted pillow sham and pillowcase, knitted hot water bottle cover, patchwork bedspread, rag floor rug. On the windowsill are fabric-covered boxes, above the bed a tapestry picture and an example of earlier, Victorian beadwork.**

BELOW: **Slipper cases, 1930s–40s.**

The bedroom was a feminine place where a man had scant opportunity to make his mark; a pair of hair-brushes on top of his tallboy or manrobe might be as far as it went. It was a woman's space to decorate and embellish, centring on the dressing table as a kind of shrine to the worship of her womanhood, and dreams of glamour.

The bedroom of the '30s, '40s and '50s was still as much a place of sickness as of slumber; many adult illnesses, in the days before antibiotics, could confine people to bed for weeks at a time. Then, too, the ways in which illness was managed were very different; people were instructed to stay in bed for relatively long periods for minor illnesses. I remember lying in my grandmother's darkened bedroom for days, forbidden to read because of the current belief I could become blinded by reading when I had measles. I read the label on the fly-spray can as best I could, over and over again. There was less faith, then, in the benefits of exercise as part of recuperation, and people were encouraged to stay lying down whereas now they'd be urged to get out of bed as soon as possible.

'To plan a feminine bedroom' is so frequently the phrase which the home-loving woman uses to describe what she wants, that I use it here — a bedroom with a freshness akin to almond blossom that lights up the landscape of early spring, or to apple blossom that blushes a little later amid greening orchards ringing with birdsong.

JULIA CAIRNS, *WOMAN'S JOURNAL*, JUNE 1950

Crocheted doily, probably 1930s.

Because people were often sick in bed, and bedrooms were typically cold places, women needed bed jackets to wear when they were sitting up in bed, toying daintily with invalid food on a tray, perhaps, and reading detective stories as my McLeod grandmother might have done, or reading romantic fiction like my grandmother Lucy did. Women's publications made much of the opportunity to create tray cloths with matching serviettes for bedridden family members (see the examples on page 145), and advised on how to make their meals look suitably enticing and ceremonial.

Bed jackets were usually knitted or crocheted, and women often made matching bed socks to wear with them to keep their feet warm in cold beds. The jackets typically tied with a girlish bow in front; knitting books made them look like a glamorous accessory, and they were an opportunity to show a range of fancy knitting stitches. Ostrich-feather stitch, bell drop-stitch and fancy drop-stitch, smocking stitch and pinecone pattern feature in a Madame Weigel bed jacket and cape pattern book I have from the '30s; my family knitted similar styles well into the 1950s. However they might also be patchwork; one of my mother's 1940s craft books has a pattern for one; and commercial patterns were available — even Vogue patterns — for fabric bed jackets. A matching hot-water-bottle cover would have been a triumph; these, too, were popular before electric blankets became common, and many patterns were available for these as well.

Rag rugs were suitable bedroom coverings for the dream cottage; I have one made from old dress fabrics. Bedspreads could have been embroidered, quilted or patchwork throughout this period, and some wool-lined patchwork ones would have been heavy enough to double as blankets.

Women embroidered their own pillowcases, their sheets less often, and they lavished embroidery on cotton pillow shams. Where bedspreads were not long enough to cover the pillows, pillow shams concealed the pillows, ironed and immaculate. They were removed at bedtime, folded, and replaced neatly in the morning. Beneath the sham a pillowcase might have been in need of laundering, but it was concealed by day; women were loath to wash linen too often, because of the labour involved in washing and drying it.

Embroidery transfers, probably for lingerie

A homemade and decorated nightdress case sat on top of many beds, and women often made decorative handkerchief sachets and stocking bags that could be out on display. A woman might embroider pictures for her bedroom wall, and her dressing table and tallboy gave her plenty of opportunity to display further embroidery, crochet and tatting skills. She might well make her own dressing gown, which would hang behind her bedroom door, along with a homemade linen bag. With wardrobe space typically meager, and a woman's wardrobe usually not extensive, out-of-season clothes could be placed in a large, specially made sealable cloth bag attached to a coat hanger that could be hung in a cupboard out of the way. I have a homemade fabric pomander or lavender-bag container designed to dangle from the neck of a coat hanger to perfume clothing stored in this way. Coathangers, too, were often padded and decorated with dress-making fabric.

The dressing table, a shrine to femininity, would invariably display a set of one large doily with two matching smaller ones. My grandmother loved to crochet; she made such dressing-table sets for every one of her female relatives, and always had one on her own dressing table. Tallboys and chests of drawers had yet more large oval or rectangular doilies on top. Also on the dressing table might be a homemade pincushion, perhaps with a china figurine sewn into it, like my mother's; daintily covered talcum-powder and face-powder containers, with separate covers for powder puffs; embroidered or felt-worked comb cases and mirrors; and home-decorated boxes — possibly fabric covered — for the woman of the house's jewellery.

A woman sat in front of her dressing-table mirror to see her own reflection; often she could manipulate side mirrors to examine her hairstyle. Her reflection would be framed by her own decorative work, sitting in front of her on display, and she could well be wearing even more

Embroidered handkerchief case, 1930s.

of it. Watching her from a small chair might be a boudoir doll she had made; I have a 1920s pattern for an elegant version. These dolls were not intended as children's toys, but as a grown woman's decorative touch; the dolls were sophisticated fashion plates or fantasy figures made and dressed by their owners. I've seen a 1930s reference to a fashionable woman carrying such a doll, dressed identically to herself, in public as a novel and witty accessory.

The houses of the '30s, '40s and '50s had fewer bedrooms, and smaller rooms, than houses do today. People were forced to share bedrooms with brothers and sisters, and children might also share rooms with ageing relatives who lived with their family; I did not have a bedroom of my own until my mother moved to the city, when the '50s had ended. Maybe this lack of privacy, which was common, and the few possessions people then owned, made them enjoy the few things they had, and drew their eye to the detail of a piece of embroidered cloth in a more appreciative way than we are used to.

ABOVE: **Knitted tea cosy, 1950s.**

RIGHT: **Novelty insulators for hot teapot handles, 1930s.**

THE KITCHEN

When I'm nostalgic for my grand-mother's house, it's her kitchen that I remember most vividly. I spent much of my childhood there, and it was the friendly social centre of her home.

Her house had been built in the 1920s, so the kitchen was the size of a modest dining room by today's standards, with a built-in coal range and its mantelpiece in pride of place. A varnished rimu gate-leg table and chairs, usually only half-extended, were fully opened on the rare days when her sisters and their families came into town from the country. On those days everybody would eat meat pies from a bakery, with tomato sauce and bread and butter, for lunch. This was a treat.

A small room led off this area to the combination pantry and scullery where food was stored, dishes were washed, and crockery and cookingware were kept. There was no refrigerator until the end of the '50s, when an electric oven was also installed. Fresh meat was kept in a hanging safe outside, under a walnut tree. Milk had to be purchased fresh every day, and ice cream had to be bought immediately before it was eaten. We didn't have it often.

ABOVE AND RIGHT: **An assortment of handworked teapot stands for protecting surfaces (such as table tops) from heat.**

Alongside the coal range was the hot-water cupboard. The coal range warmed the household's water, and my grandmother did all her cooking on it, as most New Zealand women did until well into the 1950s. Sometimes I slept in the room behind this cupboard, sharing it with my grandmother's boarder Ngaire, and the sound of the heated water bubbling through the wall was soothing. Through the wall, around the gate-leg table, my family's voices rose and fell, and the radio was a constant background noise until they went to bed themselves.

The wooden mantel radio, on its separate shelf, was permanently set to 2ZB as my grandmother ironed by day in the kitchen, listening to serials like 'Portia Faces Life' and 'Doctor Paul', and — unfailingly — to Aunt Daisy. There was no telephone; that came at the very end of the 1950s, and it was a long time before people stopped shouting into it to make

sure their voices would cross long distances. Every other room in the house stayed cold and unheated; even if we'd wanted to turn heaters on, there were no power points in them. Visitors sat in this kitchen when they called; the real sitting room was usually rented out. The lino was chipped in the kitchen, and I tugged at small holes in the wallpaper. The room was welcoming, and somebody was always busy in it. My grandmother spent a good deal of her long life there.

Some days were still set aside as baking days in my childhood, when my mother and grandmother cooked at the coal range all day, filling cake tins with cakes and biscuits that would be expected to stay edible for rather a long time. I always enjoyed jam-making days, too. We'd catch a bus to Greytown, walk to a berry farm, fill our buckets, then catch the bus home again. It was a long walk from the bus stop to our place with the heavy berries, and we had to work

quickly because berries are so perishable. There were no fancy, genteel cloth covers on our jars such as you now see in magazine illustrations.

On other days my young uncle played at the table; he had his toy cars, or my grandmother and I played Scrabble or draughts, or made scrap-picture albums. Perhaps surprisingly, considering how central the kitchen was in the household, there was only a small range of domestic textile crafts evident there, though what there was, was in everyday use.

There was always a decorative cloth put out on the kitchen table at mealtimes and teatimes; it was my job as a child to shake the crumbs off it afterwards for the birds. My grandmother often used a decorative patterned tea towel for a tea cloth, too, and an especially pleasing embroidered tea towel might have been put out informally for a guest in this

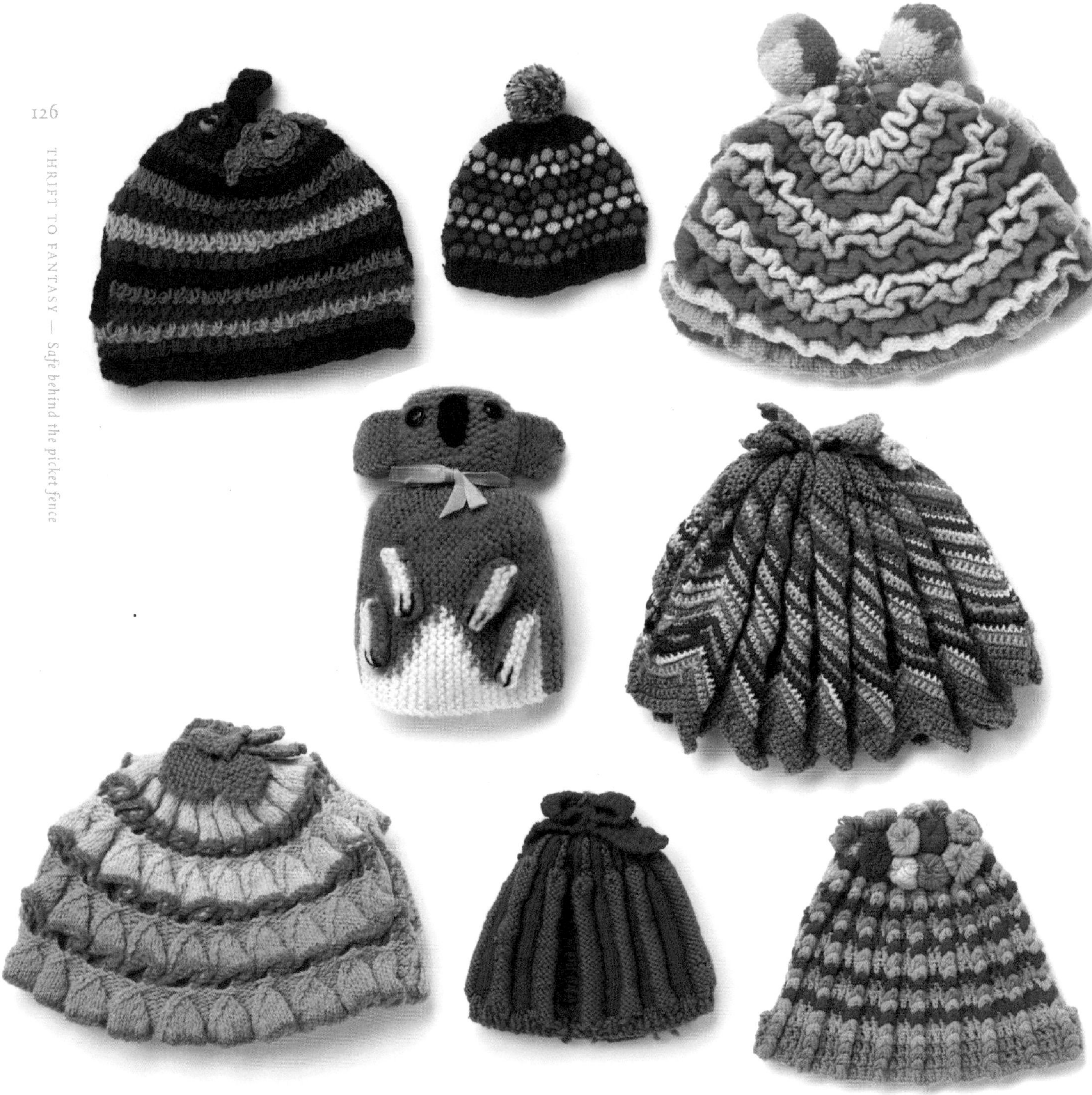

Cheerful knitted tea cosies were created in great variety for everyday use, and some patterns from this era are still being made. The koala bear cosy is a reminder that there was much travel between New Zealand and Australia during the 1930s–50s, second only to the volume of travel between New Zealand and Great Britain.

Pot mitts in variety, some evidently intended only as kitchen show-pieces, typically incorporate sacking backs and recycled curtain or dress fabrics, or use recycled woollen fabric as wadding.

way. In regular everyday use in the kitchen were knitted tea cosies, pot mitts, oven cloths and pot holders — often made from sacking trimmed with bright fabric — and beaded sugar and milk-jug covers. Superior examples of these were reserved for use when visitors came, as were more elaborately embroidered tea cloths. The women in my family wore aprons as a matter of course when they were cooking or preparing food; cheerful cotton ones were in constant everyday use to protect their clothing.

Special cheery tray cloths were reserved for times when family members were sick in bed. Sometimes these were embroidered with matching table napkins, and sometimes they were made from scraps of bright curtain fabric. Meals placed on attractive china were carried triumphantly into the sick person's room, with a miniature vase of flowers on the tray as well. Other decorative tray cloths were made for carrying breakfast in bed to a family member or guest; they are embroidered with cheery morning greetings.

LEFT: Kitchen teas were a popular way of celebrating an engagement during these decades, and kitchen decorations — such as bright pictorial tea towels which could be pinned to the wall — were popular presents exchanged between the women who attended them. This doll figure from the '30s must have been a present of this kind. Its 'head' is a wire-handled dish washer with densely looped cotton where today there would be a piece of sponge. The face of an '18th-century' man, a kind of town crier, has been cut out and stuck to a wooden spoon, which is attached to the wire washer. The 'body' has then been wrapped in a tea towel, dish cloth, and a duster made from a scrap of curtain fabric, all of which form the figure's 'clothes', tied on with strips of sheer kitchen curtain fabric. A handwritten verse attached to this with ribbon reads:

Kitty Kitchen
You stir your porridge with my face,
And with my apron dust the place,
Wash up the dishes with my shawl,
This strongly made and not too small,
My dress you see is not a hobble,
'Twill dry your glass without much trouble,
But if you want a mop instead,
You'll find one in my wooden head,
Altho' my hair has turned quite white,
I'll work for you both day and night.

The woman who received this thrifty homemade gift stored it away untouched for more than 50 years before she died; she shifted house during the Depression, and never unpacked some of her textile possessions. We can only suppose that the idea of using a male face was considered funny at the time, because men did not do housework; the gift could have been an ironic comment from an older woman to a bride — perhaps this woman — about what marriage really held in store.

Alone we are born
And die alone;
Yet see the red-
gold cirrus
Over snow-
mountain shine.

THE SITTING ROOM

I had little experience of formal sitting rooms when I was a child. The room intended for that purpose in my grandmother's house was given over to a boarder for most of those years, and few of my relatives had a formal area set aside; they all seemed to live in kitchen/dining areas, as my mother and I did in our little two-roomed bach. Four people at my mother's small dining table almost filled the room, and her primitive electric oven was barely large enough to bake a cake.

I remember sitting rooms, however, in the larger houses where my mother worked for wealthier women as a housekeeper in the 1950s. There was a lot of floral chintz, polished mahogany, and fancy china on display there as well as in my family's homes, but there might also be a liquor cabinet —

unknown in my family circle — or crystal decanters of sherry and whiskey on view, with crystal goblets beside them, and a lace tablecloth permanently spread out on a mahogany dining table which was almost never used. Many doilies which survive from this period may well have been luncheon sets intended for formal use on such tables, too. My mother's copy of *Gifts You Can Make Yourself* explains that they 'lend grace and dignity to the table'.

In the living rooms my family visited, a china cabinet invariably had pride of place, with crocheted doilies on top of it. The doilies had a practical purpose as well as a decorative one; they were intended to sit under vases of flowers, protecting the French polish from pollen or drops of water. These were rooms where the curtains were drawn unless people were in them; there was an obsession with not letting furniture get sunlight on it, causing its upholstery to fade. The rooms were usually a little stuffy and unwelcoming as a result, and behaviour was accordingly often stilted and self-conscious.

Craft books and magazines of this period encouraged ordinary women to employ a wide range of craft traditions to decorate their living and sitting areas, from making their own loose covers for major upholstered pieces of furniture to creating artificial flowers to keep in home-decorated vases which were, in fact, painted jam jars, and to sewing curtains and fabric lampshades.

I have found a wide range of embroidered cushion covers which were obviously intended for such areas, where they would be subject to relatively light use. Rag rugs would have been useful for decorating and furnishing these areas, too, along with hand-worked table runners and cloths designed in part to protect polished wooden surfaces, and in part to prettify. I have some embroidered antimacassars from the '30s; these cloths were placed over high upholstered chair backs to protect them from men's hair oil, which was still in widespread use through to the '50s. Women worked wall pictures in tapestry and other forms of needlework, and tapestry-fronted wooden fire screens and piano stools were popular in the 1930s and '40s.

All homes had some formal occasions when the housewife's best handwork was produced, whether in a designated sitting room or otherwise. Formal meals might be few in the course of a year, and my family almost never entertained anyone who was not related to them, but we had embroidered tablecloths starched and set aside for those few times. Tea parties were a far more common form of less formal entertaining, and they involved a range of specially devised textile objects, each of which showed a woman's needlework and textile skills to an appreciative and critical audience of other women.

RIGHT: **Tea has been prepared with my grandmother's everyday china. The tablecloth is a square of hemmed curtain fabric, and the felt cosy is worked with native Australian flowers. The knitted cushion is from the 1930s. The rag rug may predate that.**

LEFT: **A miniature rag rug, backed with sacking, was never used by its makers.**

Linen bag for dirty laundry, 1930s.

THE LAUNDRY
AND BATHROOM

Our laundry — at my grandmother's — was called the washhouse. In reality it had several functions, only one of which was washing clothes; it was the place where she stored fruit from her small orchard and her vegetable crops, and where she kept her gardening tools. Its use was unchanged throughout the '30s, '40s and '50s; there would be no washing machine until 1960.

There were large twin laundry tubs, in which I was sometimes bathed when I was very small, and between them stood a wringer which was turned by hand. Nearby was the copper. A fire had to be lit beneath it to heat the water for laundering; washing was immersed in that soapy water and, rinsed in one of the twin tubs, wrung out into the other, then hung out to dry. Some especially dirty washing was also rubbed clean by hand with Sunlight soap on a wooden washing board. Doing the washing took all day; it was such a chore that people were expected to change only one sheet a week, and have only one bath towel each week to see them through; we wore our clothes until they were truly dirty by today's standards.

STARCH: Mix one tablespoon laundry starch with ½ teaspoon borax and a little cold water. Add one quart boiling water, stirring all the time. Stir in ½ teaspoon fat or paraffin oil and boil 5 minutes. Use while hot, diluting if necessary.

HOUSEHOLD SOAP: Eight lb dripping, 1½ lb caustic soda, 1½ lb resin, ½ lb borax, 1 small packet soap flakes, 20 pints water. Put all into copper, except borax and soap flakes, and boil 1 hour. Then just before it goes off the boil, add borax and soap flakes. Leave in copper until next day.

TOILET SOAP: Boil together for ½ an hour, or until soap is stringy, 4 lb clarified fat, 12 oz caustic soda, 7 pints water, 2 inches ordinary candle. When nearly ready add 1 bottle coconut oil, 1 tablespoon each glycerine and citronella. Pour into washtub and leave to set.

NEW ZEALAND TRUTH COOKERY BOOK, 1957

ABOVE: **Stockings were expensive, and this embroidered stocking bag from the 1930s–40s could have been intended either for storing clean stockings or those which needed to be washed, safe from sharp objects which could cause snags or ladders.**

RIGHT: **This laundry apron from the 1940s–50s was designed to hold clothes pegs when hanging out the washing.**

Women had special aprons set aside for doing laundry work, usually hessian or sacking, often with a large front pocket for holding pegs. They also made decorative peg bags to hold the wooden clothes pegs that were in everyday use.

Laundering involved forgotten arts: the embroidery, lace and other domestic handwork had to be washed carefully by hand, dried, then starched and ironed with skill before it was fully dry. Starching was a finely judged and delicate exercise; starched work had to be ironed at just the right point of dampness to get the desired crisp finish. Women had to know to iron embroidery from the back to keep its profile; they had to know how not to tear delicate lace. Pieces I have collected from this era remained as pristine and stiffly starched as they were when they were placed in airing cupboards decades before, never to be used again. Some women dried their white handwork outside on the grass to whiten it, and blue bags were commonly thrown in to be boiled with sheets to make them whiter.

Because washing was not done every day, decorative homemade laundry bags were in common use. They were used for gathering soiled personal laundry items and keeping them together until there were enough of them to justify doing a wash. Laundry bags for personal items were typically kept in bedrooms. Women often had a smaller laundry bag there as well, for dirty stockings which had to be washed gently by hand. 'Soiled stockings have a dreadful habit of accumulating at a rapid rate, and in nine cases out of 10 are dumped from one place to another, for very rarely is a place provided for them where they can be stowed away until washday,' reads one pattern for a stocking bag, revealing that women then, as now, can be untidy. Stockings were expensive — and hard to get in wartime — so they warranted being stored, when clean, in yet more bags specially made for that purpose.

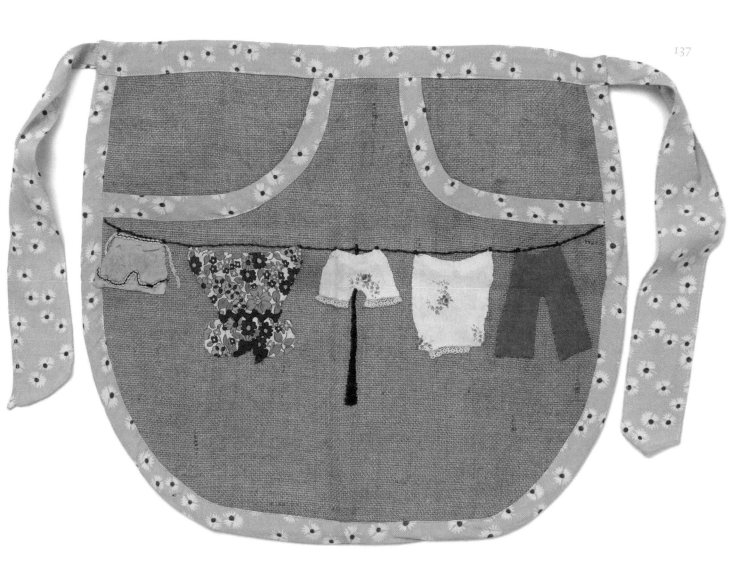

Laundry bags came in an imaginative range of styles, often using up scrap fabric from other sewing projects. They might hang behind bedroom doors from the hook reserved for dressing gowns, or they might have had a coat hanger incorporated into them so that they had more display potential; they were also easier to slip items into than a bag gathered with ordinary tape. Such bags had a front opening to slip soiled items into, and often unbuttoned at the bottom at washing time.

There was a certain amount of coyness evident in dealing with women's soiled underwear and stockings; that may have something to do with the lack of privacy which was common to many New Zealand homes, as well as with personal modesty. An example of that is a laundry bag based on a wooden hand-painted doll figure (shown in the room on page 116). The doll is dressed in a style that evoked the popular idea of the 18th century in the '30s; her skirt has a version of panniers gathered above it to each side, and she has a lace fichu on her bodice. Soiled laundry was secreted into her skirt, which is a gathered bag; her dress seems to be made from eiderdown chintz. The general impression would have been that she was a decorative toy.

Home-knitted clothing, like silk stockings and knickers, required special care. It was washed gently by hand in soapy water, rinsed, then rolled in old towels to get rid of excess water. My family would then place these pullovers or cardigans, laid out flat, between more old towels, sandwich the lot between layers of newspaper, and place them under household rugs — we had no wall-to-wall carpet — to dry on the floor in the warm living area. Women's homemade dresses and blouses had their own detachable pads, usually made from matching fabric, which were roughly stitched in place under the armpit, washed separately, then sewn back in place again. The idea was that these would become sweat-stained rather than the garment itself, which could well be made from a fabric that was unwashable because of dye run. Also, the pads could be laundered when they began to smell of perspiration, but the whole garment did not have to be washed. This was important with 1930s crepes in particular, which were difficult to handle when wet; they shrank to half their normal size, and had to be expertly ironed when still very damp to return them to their correct size; they were also apt to become water-stained if they were accidentally splashed. Other fashionable fabrics could not be washed at all; their dye ran.

RIGHT: **Embroidered duster holder, 1930s.**

Our washhouse walls were bare timber, and my grandmother's sacking rag bag hung from a nail there, alongside other bags holding preserving jar lids, pieces of string, spring bulbs and other odds and ends. I don't remember her having a bag specifically for holding dusters and rags for cleaning, but these seem to have been a popular needlework project. I have one from the '30s which features a nursery-rhyme figure of a woman who seems to have set out in a wicker laundry basket to dust — or sweep — the sky. I find it hard to equate this image with the adult domestic duties the bag was intended for; perhaps it was a child's handwork project, or perhaps it reflects a common playful theme in these household textile crafts, in which a housewife expresses herself as a young girl might. It seems likely to me that such a duster bag would have been on display in laundry areas, where cleaning products and rags were kept.

The bathroom gave women limited scope for textile handwork; in the late '50s my grandmother made crocheted tortoises for the children in her extended families; they held a cake of soap inside them, and were intended as a facecloth substitute at bath time. My mother embroidered the ends of her bath towels and face cloths with lines of decorative stitches. Women also embroidered small hand towels for guests' use; these were usually made from a fabric like huckaback, rather than towelling. Some of these hand towels were also trimmed decoratively with floral fabric left over from dressmaking.

Some women made their own sponge bags. These might range in ambition from a quilted example from this period made from a scrap of floral chintz, to simpler bags such as one with a simple tape closure which is made from fashionable leftover '50s dress fabric.

The rituals of teatime

In my childhood world there was no beverage but tea. Its role was pivotal in our lives, its ceremonies religiously observed. Coffee was Bushells coffee and chicory essence, which came in a bottle kept at the back of the cupboard, and was only ever used to flavour icing for an apple cake, a family recipe that my mother baked for shearers. There was, as yet, no instant coffee. One of my aunts once made a coffee-flavoured pavlova; it was discussed, much as a landing by Martians might have been, and was generally held to be sophisticated, probably, but too daring an experiment to ever repeat.

More sophistication — coffee, after all, was drunk by foreigners — came to Masterton in the '50s in the form of the Calypso coffee lounge. We walked past it mystified, but never entered. An artistic and racy aunt finally opened The Coffee Pot in Carterton, where she, too, served coffee. So scandalous was this that her daughters were set to work to wash the graffiti insults off the shop front regularly. Only when instant coffee arrived did my family start to drink coffee, but somehow it never took on as tea did. My mother befriended Dutch immigrants, purchased a Delft style, wall-mounted coffee grinder to make the real stuff, then forgot about it. We were tea people.

LEFT: **Embroidered teatowels featuring motifs of teatime.**

Many women did not have refrigerators in this period, and preventing flies from spoiling food was an ongoing problem. Special covers for milk jugs and sugar bowls were fashioned from netting or similar fabric, or crocheted in a variety of ingenious ways and weighed down around the edges with shells or glass beads. One popular pattern featured a crocheted teacup and saucer in the centre; my grandmother was one of many women who crocheted a version of it (see top right and bottom left covers). Another novelty crocheted cover in my collection depicts a cat playing with a ball. Some covers were worked around a wire frame which must have been designed to perfectly fit the top of a sugar bowl. Their ribbon decoration and dainty loop handles suggest they were reserved strictly for best — and maybe were never used by their makers.

We drank a great deal of tea. We had it with breakfast, for morning tea, with lunch, for afternoon tea, and after our evening meal. More often than not we drank tea before bed. I cannot imagine what it would have been like for my family in wartime, when tea was rationed to two ounces a week per person; rationing lasted from 1942 until 1948. The suffering must have been universal, since New Zealanders normally consumed about seven pounds a head of tea each year, counting children.

Tea was always made properly in a teapot, and it would have seemed indecent if that teapot were not clothed in a homemade tea cosy when it came to the table. Tea was served without fail on a tea cloth, on the dining table. For family use we'd have a printed cotton cloth most often, but there were cloths displaying graduated levels of handwork, with the most heavily

Embroidered tray cloths, 1930s–40s.

LEFT: **Patchwork tea cosy, 1930s.**

RIGHT: **These 'doll' tea cosies would have been reserved for special occasions, to impress guests. I have a pattern for these from the 1930s.**

embroidered ones qualifying for truly formal morning and afternoon teas with people we wished to impress. Such formal tea parties, however, could only be conducted in a sitting room, otherwise they'd lack appropriate gravity.

I can remember tea parties in the '50s, tea trolleys laden with best china and an assortment of homemade cakes and biscuits. I was only ever allowed three items, one of which must be plain or savoury, and only one piece of cream cake. Women dressed up for such tea parties; formal dinners were unknown in our world, and these were the only form of serious entertaining known to us. I expect it was much the same for most people during these three decades; 'Around the Editor's Tea Table' was the title of the editor's editorials in the English *Woman's Magazine*, and the illustration shows all the guests wearing hats, seated around a correctly laid-out table. Tea was the means to serious socialising; even the telephone was not immediately available to everyone, so tea parties must have been a valued way of getting to talk to women other than immediate family and neighbours.

The hostess of a tea party would wear a smart dress, stockings and high-heeled shoes, and be fully made up and corseted even if she was also wearing a frilly apron. Her guests would dress up for the occasion, too; as often as not they had to arrive by public transport, because few people had cars, so a good deal of time was set aside on the day for the event.

ABOVE: These sandwich doilies from the 1930s–40s were designed to be placed under sandwiches on a long plate for formal tea parties.

RIGHT: Embroidered tea cosy covers like these slipped over a padded inner shape, and were used for formal tea times in the 1930s–40s.

Nothing could compete, handwork-wise, with the formal dressing-up of the tea table and tea trolley. For this, special work was produced from storage — in the hot-water cupboard in our case. It was taken out almost as seriously as altar cloths would have been, and existed only for ceremonial purposes. The quality of this handwork would be an indication of the quality of the woman who made it; refinement and skill would be noticed and appreciated by others. It would also be silently noted by the guests whether the handwork was homemade or merely bought.

Use of this special handwork, which often echoed popular decorative themes in china, was an extravagant gesture: every woman present knew the labour involved in making these things, and the care taken with their laundering and ironing. Everyone knew that a hostess risked ruining a beautiful cloth if she accidentally spilled tea or milk as she poured — many old tea cloths seem to have been discarded, however beautiful they were, when they were stained — nothing but perfection was permissible, and the stain was doubtless a source of constant heartbreak even as a hostess tried to hide it from critical eyes by covering it with a sugar bowl or a plate of scones.

The tea-party tea trolley had large, matching embroidered doilies for both levels, and the tea table had one of the household's best embroidered tea cloths laid out on it. A light, embroidered throw covered both before the guests arrived, to keep flies off the food and the immaculately clean best china. Sugar bowls and milk jugs, too, had their own beaded and crocheted covers, in infinite variety, to keep the flies off, and especially fine examples were reserved for company. Women produced handworked stands for the teapot and hot-water jug, to protect the table beneath from heat, and made quaint holders so they didn't burn themselves on hot handles (see page 123).

Special hand-worked hostess aprons were made and worn on occasions such as these. They were strictly decorative, usually quite impractical — fully crocheted, perhaps, or light organdie — and they reinforced the idea of playfulness that characterised much of women's domestic textile work.

Plates of little sandwiches and cakes were covered with special embroidered doilies before food was arranged decoratively on top. Some women embroidered coasters to place teacups on, and also provided dainty embroidered napkins. Women made special scone holders which were only ever likely to see service on special occasions such as these. They were practical as well as decorative; scones are wrapped in cloth when they leave the oven to keep them soft and to help retain warmth.

Pride of place, however, went to the tea cosy. Everyday tea cosies might have been knitted or crocheted from wool, but for tea parties a novelty tea cosy, or one worked in a less practical way, would be brought out to set the more formal tone of the table. All were designed to be practical — they helped keep the tea hot by providing insulation — but many must also have been intended as talking points, a way of breaking the ice, perhaps, between women who did not know each other intimately.

The final touch after a tea party would have been embroidered tea towels, on display to impress any guest who offered to help wash up afterwards in the kitchen. These were intended to give the artless impression, no doubt, that life in the household was one of constant refinement.

LEFT: **Felt Pinocchio doll, 1940s.**

RIGHT, TOP: **Embroidered felt elephant brooch, actual size, 1930s.**

RIGHT, BOTTOM: **Felt kangaroo toy, 1930s. Similar designs of kangaroos and rabbits were often used as pincushions and needle holders.**

Children, animals . . . and the royals

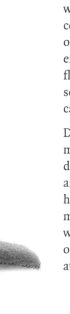

I **was one** of 21,255 girls born in New Zealand in 1949: my mother, at over 21 and under 25 years old, was by then in the biggest age group of mothers. Her hand-worked maternity layette for me was immaculate. It included, of course, several viyella versions of the Plunket Society nightie, embroidered with pink and blue flowers, and I regurgitated onto soft, home-sewn bibs topped with cambric, and trimmed with lace.

Despite the careful preparation of my immaculate layette, my father did not turn up to take my mother and me home from the nursing home; their time together as a married couple pretty well ended where I began. Like many children of this era, my life would be lived at varying points between grim reality and the elusive ideal, but nobody could fault my wardrobe.

The handwork women produced for their children in the '30s, '40s and '50s is evidence of how central motherhood was to their lives, and the importance of displaying their sewing skills as part of the proof of their maternal competence. With the example of royalty as the perfect family constantly before her in magazines, books and newspapers, my mother competed at such skills, as thousands of other women did, with widely published photographs of the growing Prince Charles and Princess Anne. Their outfits were her template for childish elegance, and the studio baby photographs of my childhood seem to be an imitation of what she saw of the royal family's.

I might be the child of a 'broken home' in Masterton, New Zealand, but my mother could sew and knit every bit as well as 'Crawfie' (Royal nanny Marion Crawford) and any of her ilk; my baby clothes were daintily smocked and embroidered crepe de Chine and lace-trimmed, just as theirs were. The major differences between us — money, rank, marital status of our parents — were mere details.

Most of the clothes children wore were homemade, knitted or sewn by their mothers. Garments were let down and let out to make them last longer, as had been the case in my grandmother's time. In my childhood a let-down hem which did not match the fading colours of the rest of a child's dress was a

familiar sight, as was too-small knitwear stretched tightly as a child waited for their mother to knit something new.

My mother can't have been alone in her fantasies about emulating royalty. Following the abdication of Edward VIII in 1936, and George VI's coronation in 1937, the new king's family life was being presented as reassuringly exemplary when I was born; the Commonwealth had seen what happened when an unmarried king threw everyone into confusion. The young princesses Elizabeth and Margaret were written about in adulatory terms in the '30s; a child's apron in my collection (shown on page 164) is embroidered with the image of both an English rose and H.R.H. Princess Elizabeth — looking grumpy — just as others I have from that time depict Disney's Snow White and Mickey Mouse. These aprons for little girls suggest the semi-fictional, idealised realm occupied by the royal family, characters in a distant real-life drama which survived into the '50s as the Queen formed her own family.

Embroidered children's aprons must have been popular; they may have been worn in junior school — one Semco apron template I have is labelled 'school apron' — and it appears that little girls often embroidered their own stencilled pictures in simple outline stitches; many of these aprons are crudely done. Other completed children's aprons I have show a pixie among flowers — English children's books were crawling with pixies at this time — a circle of pale skinned little girls playing 'ring-a-rosy', and pet animals. These children's aprons were obviously as practical a solution to the problem of protecting clothing as adult aprons were, but since they were not made for boys, as far as one can tell, they also imply that little girls were being prepared for a life of inevitable domesticity. They even produced miniature aprons for their dolls.

Crawfie's biography of the Queen, carefully vetted by the royal household, was a bestseller. Marion Crawford was the Queen's governess for 17 years, and an intimate of the royal household. Her books could be found in many homes, along with pictorial accounts of the Queen's coronation, souvenir china bedecked with images of English pageantry, and even handkerchiefs embroidered with the coronation coach. We and the royal family were surely united in our love of badgers and squirrels, thatched cottages and snow at Christmas: our books made London seem more familiar than Auckland, and the royal family seemed like members of our extended family.

I can't have been the only child confused at storybooks full of pictures of draught horses and dovecotes, and traditional English haystacks; with accounts of local titled people, talk of brooks, fields and meadows, and descriptions of children who exclaimed 'I say!', and 'Top hole!' There was an obvious, unsettling rift between that world — the one reflected in embroidery and handcraft imagery — and ours, but we saw nothing strange in adults calling England 'home' when they had never been there, even if it made us wonder why this place wasn't.

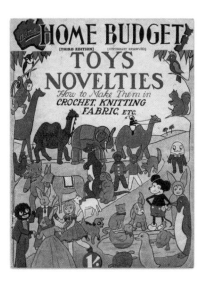

LEFT: **Embroidery transfer motif.**

ABOVE: **Publications such as this one, from the 1930s–40s, featured patterns for a range of toys and novelties for women to make as gifts, or to sell for fundraising at church bazaars.**

LEFT: **Home-made teddy bear made from woollen fabric.**

RIGHT: **A colouring book from this period gives an instructive glimpse into the way children were taught about the colonisation of New Zealand. The welcoming images of friendly Maori would have an ironic tinge to them before long.**

I have never found a child's garment from these decades with embroidered images of native birds and flowers. Women were expected to be conformists, and there was probably safety in using similar imagery and stitches to everyone else's. Also, many mothers must have been recent English immigrants, still looking homeward in their minds for what was appropriate.

A pink child's dress which could date from any time in this period has traditional English embroidery and homemade Dorset buttons. Smocking — a form of English embroidery which evolved from Saxon times — was popular for decorating both small girls' and boys' clothing. A set of embroideries worked by an Auckland woman for nursery walls in the '50s has imagery that could be from anywhere in the Commonwealth, with a row of stylised soldiers suggesting the guards at Buckingham Palace. A creative piece of appliqué work, a nursery wall hanging, shows Little Miss Muffet — from the English nursery rhyme — and the spider who frightened her. We had no nursery rhymes about ourselves.

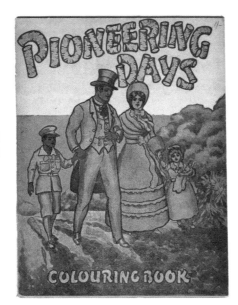

New Zealand at last! With brown, tattooed Maoris to carry them ashore, Mary clings to her doll, while John sits astride the burly shoulders of one of the Maori boatmen.

A friendly Maori leads them out to the bush where their new home is to be built. Here, the great trees have to be felled to provide timber for their home.

Women's magazines regularly featured embroidery projects, often intended for the nursery, on their covers at this time.

It's no wonder children were the focus of much creative attention during these decades. The upheaval of recent world wars evidently made both returned soldiers and their wives aspire to traditional family life, with its hopeful stability and security. The cult of the child film star Shirley Temple in the '30s — my Aunt Barbara kept paper dolls of her until she died — was surely an expression of this wish: the dimpled Temple, in her song-and-dance films, seems to have been a symbol of innocence and optimism in hard times, just as real children were to their own families.

Reality was very different from that described by Crawford, however, for many New Zealand children. If women's magazines stressed an almost militaristic approach to hygiene, diet and exercise in the care of immaculately dressed children, this must have reflected the anxiety of parents whose children could fall seriously ill at any time from common diseases of childhood which were potentially fatal, and which often swept through the country as epidemics. Careful, time-consuming hand-work carried out by their mothers must have been a way of emphasising children's value, and investing time in their futures even as they seemed uncertain.

New Zealand boasted the lowest rate of infant mortality in the world in the '30s, and gave the credit to the Plunket movement founded by Sir Truby King, which had a significant impact on child health among the European population. We did not include Maori babies in those statistics. If we had, we would have had to tell a different story.

Maori babies were dying at three times the rate of European babies as these decades began, and there would not be much of an improvement in that ratio by the time they ended. Between 1928 and 1937, 104 of every 1000 Maori children died in the first year of life, compared with 33 Europeans; a year later, as the country began to climb out of the Depression, the rate had risen to 153 Maori deaths per 1000 live births. This rate fell back to 54 per 1000 live births — still nearly three times the rate for European children — in 1958.

Whooping cough, scarlet fever and diphtheria in particular claimed many children's lives. We were also subject to poliomyelitis (polio) epidemics: between 1947, when my parents married, and 1949, the year I was born, nearly a thousand children under the age of 14 contracted the disease. There was no vaccination programme for polio — a disease which could cause paralysis and permanent disability even if it did not kill — until 1956.

Yet despite these dangers, New Zealand children grew bigger in both height and weight between 1934 and 1954. Fifteen-year-old boys gained an average of 12 kilograms, and girls 7.5. We were bigger than the English.

Despite the idealisation of childhood at this time, and the care lavished on making clothing, toys and nursery decorations for children in the cottage idyll, not all children were wanted in these times of fluctuating fortunes. Contraception was not yet reliable; members of my family still swore by vinegar douches after intercourse, and when one of my desperate great-aunts, who had seven children in nine years, had a tubal ligation, it was considered a little scandalous. Young women often remained ignorant of the facts of life, perhaps in an attempt to prolong their innocence at a time when this was culturally valued, and perhaps in the faint hope that if they didn't know how sex was done, they wouldn't do it. It didn't work.

Despite the white-wedding dreams involved in 'One day my prince will come' as the '30s began, nearly a third of all babies were conceived outside marriage. A shotgun wedding may not have been an auspicious start to married life, though it was surely preferable to having to give a baby up for adoption, the only other option for unmarried women at a time when their pregnancy was a social disgrace.

The dilemma of the 'girl in trouble' was spelt out in a short story in the English *Woman's Magazine* of June 1950. 'Fear and horror clawed at her relentlessly,' we are told of the story's heroine. 'She thought of writing to Tim; he was the only person in the world who would understand. She had started dozens of letters: "My darling Tim," and stopped there. For what was the use of writing to him? He was halfway to New Zealand in his training ship, he couldn't help.' All turns out well for our heroine, as she learns she is not an island; she owes an obligation to her family to do the right thing — and marry Tim.

Pregnant women who did not marry typically left home and went to live elsewhere until their babies were born; their families helped them to cover up what had really happened, and the babies were never to be mentioned again. In the first year of life, the death rate for illegitimate children in the early '30s was higher than it was for the babies of married women, despite overall improvements in child health. The inference is ominous.

The overall birth rate in New Zealand declined by 38 per cent between 1916 and 1935, accelerating toward the end of that period; this reflected the effect of the Depression, which caused marriages to be deferred. It shot up again after the first Labour government was elected; nearly half of all first-born babies were produced in the first year of marriage in that rush of unusual optimism, and hope that the hard times were gone. My grandmother's youngest child, my uncle Bill, was born in 1939. She must have shared the hope that hard times were over.

The poverty of the Depression told its story in abortion statistics, too, however. Deaths from abortion itself — it was illegal — and the infections associated with it peaked in 1934, when 42 women died from them. 'The stigma of a high septic abortion mortality rate lies upon New Zealand at the present time,' the *Official New Zealand Yearbook* for 1938 records, noting the average death rate from septic abortion for the five years 1931–35 placed New Zealand third highest in the list of countries for which comparable information was available.

Adoptions surged ahead that year; there were 570 children adopted, the second-highest number on record, but so did divorces, to the highest level in a decade. The yearbook did not comment on that.

Illegitimate births would rise in wartime once more, and so would divorce. A record 1191 children were adopted in 1945, as against 340 a decade earlier. A year later, 1946 was a record year for divorce. This was also the year when the 'child allowance' was introduced — payable directly to mothers.

This may have had an effect on the 'baby boom' that followed the war: the child allowance was a substantial sum at that time, and for many women it must have been the only money they had independent control of until they qualified, many years later, for universal superannuation.

In 1952 there was once again a record number of illegitimate births, 2104; only 1944 recorded more. And in 1952 there was one divorce for every 10 marriages.

Women's magazines of this period feature young widows, either in short stories, problem pages or feature articles. That reflects reality for women whose husbands had been sent to war, and who might very well not return. However, I have found no comparable mention of divorced women's problems, despite the increasing divorce rate. I suspect the cottage idyll did not allow for such a possibility.

The wheels may have been wobbly under family life in the '50s despite the outward impression of happy families and rising prosperity, and the social pressure to conform in a small society. There were 7975 divorces in 1950–54 compared with 4907 in 1936–40, an increase of 63 per cent. Well over 2000 children each year in the '50s saw their parents divorce, and were exposed to the social stigma associated with that. We do not know how many coped with having separated parents, as I did.

Divorces were reported solely in the *Truth* in my childhood. That newspaper also published details of criminal offending, like rape, which was considered too distasteful for daily newspapers to report. The analogy was easily drawn between crime and failed marriages. My mother dreaded such public exposure of her private life, as others must have done, on her own behalf as well as mine. I knew no other child in my situation in the '50s. Perhaps, like my family, they chose not to speak of it, or glossed over the subject as if the separation was a temporary arrangement, as I was told to do. Meanwhile women's magazines and the movies continued to paint a picture of ideal family life and immaculate children.

Rag doll dressed in 1940s dress fabric, and in contemporary style.

ABOVE: **Miniature squirrel is improvised from twigs, wire, wool and crash fabric.**

RIGHT: **Pair of Scotty dogs, actual size, are intended to be pinned on clothing and worn as a brooch, 1930s.**

Handcrafts may be associated with standardised imagery during this period, reflecting commonly held values, but there was leeway for individual creative expression in the making of children's soft toys, often improvised from materials at hand. Children were not, as yet, exposed to mass-produced and readily available toys, backed by sophisticated merchandising. They can't have been self-conscious about having homemade toys.

Felt toys were popular for small children, particularly felt animals; this probably reflects the popularity of talking animals in children's books at the time. None of the animals depicted in this handwork are indigenous, of course, although some would have been familiar to children as pets or pests — rabbits, dogs, cats.

A pattern for a rabbit with patch-pocket trousers seems to have been widely available in the '50s, as was another rabbit pattern which sometimes appears in a smaller version as a needle-and-pin holder; women seem to have made toys for themselves, in effect, as a popular kangaroo pattern also sometimes doubles in the same way. A felt handmade Pinocchio doll presumably dates from the '40s (page 150); Disney's animated movie was released in 1940.

Women made toys with leftover fabric, also. A Scotty dog — these were a popular decorative theme in the '30s — is made from checked woollen fabric, probably suiting, and a teddy bear is made from a soft wool fabric which is probably also left over from a dress or coat. An unusual piglet doll with an embroidered face is dressed in a frock made from leftover dress fabric which could have been worn by its child owner; so is a purchased doll in a homemade frock; these date from the '30s and '40s. A cloth doll wears a matching bonnet and dress styled much like those her owner would have worn in the '40s (page 159). There is a pattern for a doll very like it in my mother's contemporary copy of *Gifts You Can Make Yourself*.

There's more recycling of dress fabric scraps in a suite of miniature upholstered furniture made from matchboxes, covered with gingham and floral-patterned fabric; it may have been destined for a homemade doll's house. Pattern books of the era are full of ideas for knitted toys.

I went away to boarding school at the age of eight, taking with me a small pocket doll my mother had made from my Aunt Barbara's white nurse's stocking. I also took a laundry bag she had decorated by copying a picture I chose from one of my children's books. On one side it has the figure of Mickey Mouse, his trousers made from a scrap of one of my gingham school-uniform pinafore aprons, and on the other is the image of a dejected Pluto the pup. I suppose she intended this handwork to be a cheerful memento of home, a reminder that I was important to her as an individual even as I settled down to a highly regimented life among 80 other boarders. I suppose she was also content with believing I was being exposed to a long British tradition of sending young children away from home. It would be many years before I would discover that other children I lived among then were also there because of failed marriages, but at the time our parents' failure to live the cottage idyll successfully was our collective guilty secret.

Meanwhile less fortunate children ended up in children's 'homes' or orphanages. Contrary to what was generally supposed, most of these so-called orphans had living parents. Only 13 of 1301 children

in such institutions in 1943, for example, were known to have lost both parents, and just 97 were illegitimate. The implication is that many parents felt able to give up their children; 940 that year had both parents alive, and 20 married couples had abandoned newborn infants. At the start of the next century, some of these children would expose regimes of sexual abuse within those institutions.

The hidden side of the cosy toys that survive from this period, suggesting happy childhoods, was family and school violence: children were beaten at home and at school as punishment for misbehaving, as their parents had been before them. Nobody saw that as a problem: perhaps against a background where sheer survival was often the ultimate aim, such thoughts would have been an unnecessary luxury. Adults were also hard on each other, and the background of a world war may have dwarfed the significance of acts of everyday violence in the home.

Last spring I arranged some nurseries, for an exhibition. For £1.1s.9d a chauffeur-mechanic made a table with flaps and drawer, a milk-safe cupboard, two chairs, an ordinary cupboard, a stand and cradle, and a screen, complete, out of packing cases, banana crates and sacking. So a man's ingenuity overcame financial difficulties, and proved we could all afford an up-to-date nursery.

'OUR CHILD' BY GWEN ST AUBYN, WOMAN'S MAGAZINE ANNUAL, 1932

Queen Elizabeth was the first of her line to be proclaimed Head of the Commonwealth. Millions of people of many races and colours are bound not only to her but also to one another by their common allegiance. This allegiance is dependent on many factors, including mutual assistance and defence; but the one factor that gives meaning to all the rest is the affection in which the Throne is held … It is [the Queen's] job to be in a sense 'owned' by her people. No longer does the Monarch command in the old absolute way, the Sovereign is the personage who symbolises for all of us the perfection we would most like to attain.

MARION CRAWFORD,
QUEEN ELIZABETH II, 1952

This spectacular hooked wool rug was designed and made by Aucklander Lucy May Dunbar (1911–95). It is a wedding portrait of Queen Elizabeth II and her husband Prince Philip, which must have been based on a contemporary photograph. The Queen is in a cream wedding gown embellished with real diamante pieces, and the prince in a dark green dress uniform. They stand against a dramatic scarlet curtain back-ground. There is a lion rampant motif at the top left and right corners, and a crown above their heads. The Queen holds a bouquet of flowers. Mrs Dunbar was able to suggest the folds in drapery behind them, and in the Queen's clothing, as well as the steps the figures stand on, despite the obvious challenge of the medium she used. She was so skilful that she was also able to successfully convey the impression of lace in both the dress and veil. The Duke of Edinburgh's insignia is lovingly depicted in detail. The rug — which must have been intended to hang on a wall — is signed and dated 1950–52. Mrs Dunbar's proud family loaned the rug to the Auckland War Memorial Museum in 1954, where it has remained ever since. My 'Thrift to Fantasy' exhibition in 2003 was the first time this outstanding piece of women's textile art was publicly displayed. (Rug measures 1905 x 1254mm)

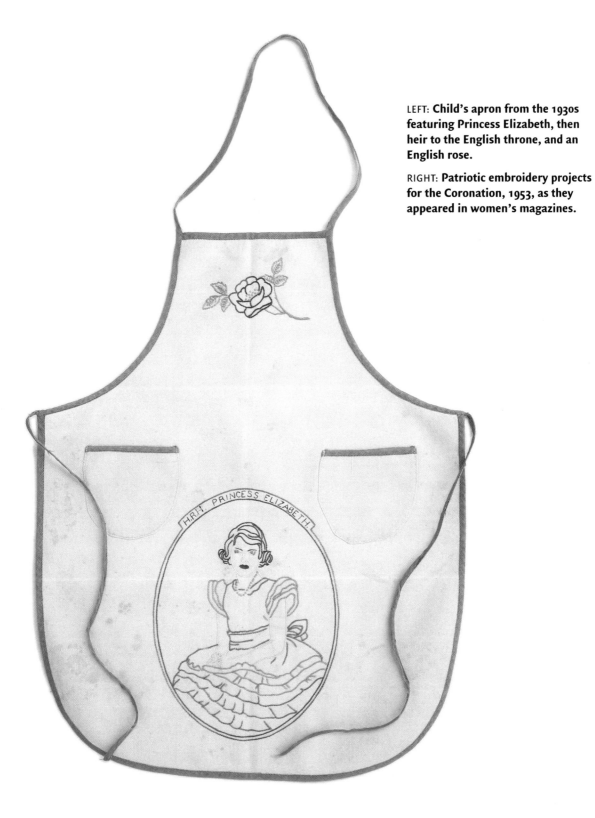

LEFT: **Child's apron from the 1930s featuring Princess Elizabeth, then heir to the English throne, and an English rose.**

RIGHT: **Patriotic embroidery projects for the Coronation, 1953, as they appeared in women's magazines.**

H.R.H. PRINCESS ELIZABETH

OUR SPECIAL CORONATION TRANSFER

*A handsome cushion in heraldic design
to make and embroider as a souvenir*

*The petals are edged with
stem-stitch and filled in with
long-and-short stitch, shading
through paler pink and
yellow to the orange centre.*

THIS month we offer our readers a beautiful embroidery transfer, specially designed for Coronation year.

In the centre is the coat of arms, with the Lion and Unicorn and the ribbon of the Garter surmounted by the Crown. Surrounding this decorative centrepiece is a border of national flowers.

To make the cushion-cover you will need : *A piece of smooth natural linen twenty-one inches square ; a piece of pink linen the same size and some extra crossway strips to match for the piping ; the following skeins of " Anchor " stranded cotton : three each of white and old gold (733), two each of deep pink (440), light blue (876), dark green (576) and salmon pink (677) ; one skein each of pale yellow (582), deep lemon (489), blue (508), spring green (777), pale salmon (542), olive green (789), cerise (586), purple (415), mauve (861), and black ; and Transfer No. 1,761.*

Iron off the transfer in the centre of the natural linen square. Then begin the embroidery, using only two strands threaded in the needle for all black embroidery, three strands for the outline of the daffodils, and the trumpet and centres, the outline and centres of the wild roses, all leaves, veins, stems, calyx, and also for the lion's tail. Use all six strands for the rest of the embroidery.

The complete design measures 16½ inches square.

*The Cushion Cover—it is piped
and backed with soft rose-pink.*

*The " Regalia " Transfer No. 1,761 is price 10d. each
copy, plus a large, stamped, self-addressed envelope, and
obtainable from WOMAN AND HOME Transfer No. 1,761,
Bear Alley, Farringdon Street, London, E.C.4.*

*Use deep pink, cerise and mauve
lazy-daisy loops for the clover
flowers and two shades of green
for the trefoil leaves.*

*The daffodil
petals are in
stem-stitch and
single stitches.*

Wife and Home

**Coronation
Transfer Offer**

Price in South Africa
and New Zealand 1/3
MONTHLY
FEBRUARY 1937

**Embroidered picture of the
coronation of King George VI and
his queen, who would later become
the Queen Mother, 1932 (private
collection).**

four

Part Four: Beyond the front gate

Exotic escapes and foreigners

ABOVE: **Embroidered square for an uncompleted project, 1930s, possibly Hungarian.**

LEFT: **Detail of embroidery.**

Of all the Dominions, New Zealand is the most isolated, and this tends to prevent rapid dissemination of new ideas which close contact with other nations is bound to bring about.

M. WINIFRED GUY, WOMAN'S MAGAZINE ANNUAL, 1934

The lure of the foreign and exotic may have been strong for those New Zealand women who dreamed of escape from the predictability of their lives, but it must have been an equally scary prospect for others. This was, after all, one of the most remote places in the world in the 1930s; we could only be reached by boat, only a very few thousand tourists made it here each year, and few New Zealand women would ever travel abroad.

That meant we were remote in more ways than one, a closed society from which significant outside influences were effectively excluded. Physical isolation was obvious, but we were equally isolated from cultures different from our own; Australia, the nearest major country, had the same language and a broadly similar cultural tradition as a

ABOVE: **Japanese needle case.**

RIGHT: **Detail of embroidered tea cloth featuring Chinese coolies with traditional pigtails, 1930s–40s.**

Commonwealth country. Real foreigners did not come as tourists in any great numbers, and our immigration policy made sure that few could come to stay.

If we looked outward at all, it was to Britain. We sought British immigrants, and were the biggest of Britain's trade customers, on a per capita basis, at the start of World War II. One way we protected that influence was through the 1928 Cinematograph Films Act, which imposed a set guaranteed percentage of British films on cinemas; another was through clothing tariffs of just 25 per cent on imported British clothing; it was 65 per cent on clothing from everywhere else. We also had a system of assisted immigration, for which only British immigrants could apply.

In the 1936 census the main 'alien' groups were Chinese (2899), Syrian (1229) and Indian (1146); by the start of World War II, just 8000 'aliens' were registered here, in a total population of 1.6 million. By 1958 a far wider range of nationalities was recorded, the largest group being the Dutch; 13,000 had arrived. There were 3530 Chinese registered in second place, an indication they were still not here in great numbers, even after nearly a century, and there were 1560 Germans in third place. We were reluctant to admit foreigners; only one refugee arrived here for every 1500 New Zealanders, compared with one per 480 people in the United Kingdom.

Foreign countries would have been places, in the minds of most women here in the '30s, '40s and '50s, where male members of their families went to fight wars, so far away they must have seemed as unreal as the movies. My Uncle George's 'naughty boy' wartime souvenir from Belgium, with a corkscrew in the obvious place for opening wine bottles, was not especially informative about the lie of the land there, but was as close as we were going to get to a cross-cultural Belgian experience. My father detested foreign food all his life because of the reek of garlic on the Italian troop ship that took him to fight in Italy. As for my mother, she gravitated toward foreigners of any description, wherever she found them. But she was unusual.

The chances of meeting foreigners during the 1930s and '40s were slim. Thanks to the Depression, the number of new immigrants from all sources plummeted and 94 per cent of all immigrants were from Commonwealth countries in any case. Assisted immigration virtually stopped between 1927 and 1947, when it started up once more, concentrating still on British migrants but also including Dutch, Austrians, Germans, Danes and Swiss — all uncomfortably Aryan in hindsight — and in 1956 we took in 1000 Hungarian refugees. It's obvious we were consciously still encouraging people of British and European stock, 'white' people, to settle here.

Most women would never travel abroad — none of the women in my extended family apart from my aunt did — and relatively few would even meet anyone from another culture other than a Maori, or perhaps a Chinese greengrocer, in person until the 1950s. Yet even Maori must have seemed like a distant reality; they were as yet confined, in the main, to rural areas, and surprisingly little was officially known about their lives; statistics for Maori were kept separate, and invariably annotated as being unreliable. There were almost no Maori living in the South Island, where it must have been easy to dismiss them from consideration.

Chinese people may have first come to follow gold rushes in the mid 19th century, but they — and they alone — had to pay a hefty poll tax if they wanted to become New Zealand citizens. Just four people of Chinese nationality made it here in 1932, and they could expect to have little impact on local handcraft traditions.

Foreigners barely feature in women's handwork, with the exception of black people, whose images I will discuss elsewhere. The only recurring exotic images I've discovered from this period are of Chinese, Mexicans and the Dutch. This did not change over 30 years.

Overseas, images of Chinese in needlework were often associated with laundry bags; the Chinese laundry was ubiquitous in countries like the United States, which came to discriminate against them less actively than we did. In this country they seem, in embroidery, to have been more associated with exotic and distant places where, truth to tell, they mostly remained.

Many New Zealanders must have formed their idea of the Chinese from the movies, where racist stereotypes were presented matter-of-factly, as well as from fear of the 'yellow peril' which, it was feared, might overrun this country if we were not vigilant. However, women would have been aware of Chinese and Japanese textiles and needlecrafts, because household linen and embroidered clothing reached here from those countries.

Mexican imagery had no threatening associations; the dancing señorita, a man in a sombrero and a quaint little burro were popular images in embroidery. I have a large embroidery transfer from about 1900, in which a dashing Spanish dancer poses with a rose between her teeth, and an illustrated example of another in the March 1937 *Woman's Journal*, but most of this work I have seen dates from the 1940s and '50s. I suspect the appeal of these figures came from Westerns, which were popular at the cinema at this time, as were cowboy comics. Mexicans often featured in Westerns; women as dark-haired (and therefore passionate, but untrustworthy) love interest, and men as duplicitous villains or humble family retainers for wealthy European ranchers.

In 1948 there were 265 Dutch people registered as aliens here, but seven years later there were 3356 Dutch New Zealanders. Our immigration law was changed in favour of the Dutch in 1950 when we entered into a special agreement with the Netherlands government. Having identified the Dutch as especially suitable for assimilation into our British-dominated culture (Protestant, hard-working, looking like us), we offered assisted passage to 55 young Dutch single men in 1950–51. My mother befriended one of these men, and went to board in his immaculately dec-orated house in Wellington. She was soon shocked to discover that she had met her first homosexual; these were innocent times for government policymakers, and not all handsome Dutch bachelors were likely to be integrated into New Zealand society by marriage.

The following year 937 Dutch men and 163 Dutch women arrived, and a year after that 2108 Dutch men with 601 Dutch women. No other nationality, outside those in the British Commonwealth, was to be invited here on such favourable terms. As a comparison, we took in

ABOVE: **'Dutch girl' tea cosy, probably from the 1950s.**

LEFT: **Detail of Mexican-themed tea cloth.**

'Dutch girl' laundry apron, intended
to hold pegs, probably from the 1950s.

an almost identical number of selected European refugees in the three years between 1949 and 1952, before that scheme ended. These people would have been displaced by World War II. It is interesting to contrast their fate with that of the Chinese, who were so actively discriminated against.

It's easy to see why Westerns were popular; they depicted a life that was in many ways similar to the colonists' here. It must have been reassuring to see Red Indians, as they were still called, endlessly lose their battles with the valiant American colonists who wanted their land. Something similar had happened here, after all, with 19th-century land confiscations, so Mexican imagery must have been associated with the originally exotic but now tamed world of colonisation as we believed it to be. Rosa, a knitted Spanish dancer (or 'dusky Spanish beauty') in a 1950s craft magazine I have was a touch of the safely exotic who could not scare a child.

Possibly as a response to the influx of new immigrants after World War II, with their many nationalities, a Lower Hutt woman made these cushion covers, in the style of Italian Assisi work, and in Mexican and Swedish themes. An attached letter written by one of her friends reads: 'This needlework was done by Mrs M.B. Campbell probably during the latter part of her life. She was born in 1884 and died in 1955. She always loved needlework, and learnt all she knew of her art from books and never had any lessons. The cushion covers represent embroidery of different countries, but the set was never completed.' The designs are worked to a large scale in thick thread, suggesting that Mrs Campbell was perhaps losing her eyesight with age, and with it the ability to do finer work.

The Dutch housewife remains a byword for housekeeping skill, and the peaked traditional Dutch headgear and clogs recur accordingly on items associated with cleanliness, like aprons and laundry accessories. Tulips, the Dutch national flower, also feature in embroidery, but they are, I suspect, more likely to be associated with Edward VIII, as they were the official flower in his coronation year, according to the *Woman's Magazine Annual*.

An influx of 100,000 American troops stationed here during World War II was the largest group of foreigners to ever come here, but it's unlikely they had much impact on women's handwork. However, my mother embroidered an autograph tea cloth during the war (page 46), and autograph quilts as well as variants like hers originated in 19th-century America.

Ordinary women would have met real, foreign-language-speaking foreigners for the first time in the '50s, and would have been more likely to be exposed, through interaction with those women, to the influence of different handwork traditions. However, most textile handwork from this time retains homely fantasy cottage and garden associations.

Depicting different nationalities in needlework may well have been a way of incorporating foreigners, with their threat of change, into New Zealand women's own way of life. Foreigners, attractively depicted in stitches, could do service on laundry bags, cushion covers and tea cloths, and we could assert a subtle dominance over them as they crept into the perimeters of our tentatively threatened world.

RIGHT: **Women in the 1930s seem to have felt the need to escape mentally into a distant fictional past as much as into exotic locations. The woman on this felt workbag, dressed in her powdered wig, has retreated there among the elements of a cottage garden, tripping along with a nosegay of flowers wrapped in satin ribbon. Unusually for felt work, her skirts have been gathered to enhance the sense of fullness in her dress. An idealised past seems to have been a comforting thought for people who were challenged by hard times and the threat of war, and was no more inaccessible in reality than foreign travel was for most New Zealand women.**

Jolly black folk

A GAME TO PLAY WITH GOLLY

TAKE A PENCIL, SHUT YOUR
EYES AND JAB AT GOLLY.
WHEN THE POINT TOUCHES THE PAGE,
OPEN YOUR EYES AND SEE WHERE YOUR PENCIL HAS LANDED.
YOU SCORE POINTS ACCORDING TO WHERE YOU HIT GOLLY.
PLAY IT WITH YOUR FRIENDS. HERE ARE THE SCORES:—

EITHER EYE	· · · · 25	MOUTH	· · · ·	20
FEET, HANDS AND HAT	· · 15	JACKET	· · · ·	10
TROUSERS	· · · · 5	ELSEWHERE	· · · ·	0

91

ABOVE: **This page from a 1950s children's book suggests a rather sinister approach to Golly. A child is asked to stab at Golly with a pencil, with premium prize points awarded for striking his eyes.**

LEFT: **Velvet golliwog, 1930s or earlier.**

We were not totally at ease. There was another side to the images of English cottage life, cottage flowers and the pale glamour girls embroidered by New Zealand women in the last great period of 'making do'.

The world of black people offered up the chance for creativity that was less inhibited in its colour range and subject matter, and at the same time, reassuringly comforting. It incorporated black people into home life as cheerful and harmless companions — like the golliwogs that were popular children's toys — just as real black people began to seem threatening in the world beyond the front gate.

THOUGH SUSAN BATHS HIM EVERY NIGHT, SHE CANNOT SCRUB HER GOLLY WHITE.

My Aunt Barbara's 1930s children's picture book suggests an attitude towards coloured people that would become embarrassing and unacceptable by the end of the century.

It appears golliwogs originated with Florence Kate Upton, who created the character of 'golliwog' in her popular children's poem of 1895, 'The Adventures of Two Dutch Dolls'. In America a tradition of black homemade dolls reflected the reality and presence of black culture there, and Upton's original golliwog is believed to have been based on a slave doll, which was later sold to raise funds to equip an ambulance in World War I.

Just how a child was supposed to feel about golliwogs was not altogether straightforward. Were they always good characters, or were they sometimes bad? If they were bad, was this determined by their colour? Enid Blyton's popular *Noddy* books featured golliwogs, and decades later her books were banned from libraries, reassessed as being racist. Other children's books featured golliwogs ambiguously as toys a child might feel safe treating with hostility unlike, say, teddy bears, who seem always to have been benign figures in the world of children. But golliwogs always have cheerful, smiling faces — they are obviously not intended to frighten a child — and with their bold colours and inventive costumes, they must have been fun to make.

The black bodies of golliwogs were a perfect foil for theatrical dress in a conformist society; they could plausibly wear curtain-ring earrings, bow ties and funny hats. Such inventiveness must have been influenced by the roles women saw black actors playing in films, often as cartoon-like characters from the deep south of America, the women dressed as black mammies, with their hair tied up in bright kerchiefs, and the men as colourful scarecrows in hand-me-down clothes. This was a period of unselfconscious 'coon humour', when black characters could still be portrayed as ignorant buffoons; New Zealand cartoonist Trevor Lloyd earlier belonged to that tradition, presenting Maori as loveable, opportunistic rogues.

An outstanding example of black stereotyping was the character played by Hattie McDaniel, the first black woman to receive an Oscar as Best Supporting Actress for the 1939 film *Gone With the Wind*. She played the role of Scarlet O'Hara's Mammy. When McDaniel died in 1952 the Hollywood cemetery of her choice refused to bury her because she was black. Such overt racism was foreign to New Zealand culture.

On the other hand, George Gershwin's '30s musical *Porgy and Bess*, with its all black cast, was a hit in America, and many black artists were appreciated and admired. But the relationship of Europeans with blacks and other races was often uneasy all over the world in these three decades, as power began to shift. Humour based on the European perception of them, and the wish to stereotype them, may have masked nervousness as blacks — then called 'negroes' — began to assert their civil rights, and successfully challenge colonial powers.

In 1947, the Mau Mau rebellion in Kenya, a Commonwealth country like New Zealand, led to years of fighting between factions loyal to the colonial administration and those seeking independence. Britain imposed a state of emergency in 1952. The killing of Europeans caused many to leave the country; 32 white settlers died.

The Belgian Congo became Zaire in 1960 after a violent black-led revolution which must also have shocked European colonists everywhere. A year later, South African Prime Minister Hendrik Verwoerd withdrew his country from the Commonwealth. There had been international outrage at the 1960 Sharpeville Massacre, when South African police opened fire on protesting Africans, killing 69 and injuring a further 180. Verwoerd's party had introduced its internationally condemned policy of apartheid in 1948.

All of these events and tensions must have seemed ominous, if distant, to European New Zealanders in a country with a significant indigenous culture. And there were more, albeit less violent, signs of power shifts in race relations.

The black civil rights movement in America won a crucial victory in 1954 when the Supreme Court ruled that segregation in public schools was unconstitutional. A year later, Rosa Parks refused to give up her bus seat to a white passenger, sparking a boycott of buses by blacks in Montgomery, Alabama until buses were also desegregated in 1956.

In 1957 Little Rock, Arkansaw, saw nine black students blocked from entering a local school by crowds of white protesters. President Dwight Eisenhower sent the National Guard to intervene on the students' behalf.

English people seem to have the knack of making a home anywhere. Given a few of their personal belongings, a couple of chairs, some chintz and their own cheerful dispositions, automatically and often unconsciously they manage to create a home atmosphere as soon as they find four walls in which to do it. Perhaps that is one of the reasons why the Britisher abroad is so successful in his work among native races; even on the edge of the world he is happy — he is at ease because he is home.

'HOME LIFE' BY MRS WILLOUGHBY BULLOCK, *WOMAN'S MAGAZINE ANNUAL*, 1937

All of these major stories about racial conflict were reported in local newspapers, and would have featured in newsreels which played at New Zealand cinemas before television arrived here in the '60s. Such news was in the background of everyday life, however distant. More benignly, the '50s also saw a rise in the popularity of black-inspired music like calypso and rock and roll, and imagery of black people resurfaced on tableware and kitchenware, where it had been popular in the '30s, as well as in domestic china. Black could be chic.

I see the black people imagery created by New Zealand women in their textile crafts as a way of taming frightening events, just as, to some extent, I see European women's domestic-craft traditions as their way of taming the world. While we believed we had perfect race relations here, heading towards complete integration through intermarriage, and overt racism had never been sanctioned in New Zealand, overseas events must have demonstrated the potential for what could happen if anything went wrong.

An outstanding felt workbag from the '30s features dancing black female figures outside an African hut, their costumes carefully beaded in a tribute to African beadwork. The bag would, of course, have been carried and used by a European woman practising her own craft traditions. I see this workbag as an acknowledgment of mutuality; women of all races practise their own domestic crafts; but it is also a subtle assertion of dominance that was harmless in its intention, and probably also unconscious. The white woman carried the black women, after all. It was she who was in control.

Many golliwogs — most of mine are probably from the 1950s — were hand-knitted by mothers, making them soft and pleasing toys for small children to play with. One of mine sports an early Rastafarian hairdo. Women seem to have used scrap wool to dress golliwogs; they often wear strong, random mixtures of colours. They also used scraps of fabric — cotton, even velvet — to make and dress cloth golliwogs, one of whom (page 186) wears a 1950s child's miniature straw party hat.

LEFT: **Black ballet dancers perform on this 1930s workbag, an awkward example of attempting to blend European and black culture.**

ABOVE: **Felt workbag, African theme, 1930s.**

ABOVE: **Black 'clothespeg' doll, 1930s–40s.**

RIGHT: **'Rainy-day' black cloth doll, 1950s.**

An especially crude black golliwog female (right) seems to be a 'rainy-day' doll improvised by a child and her mother roughly from fabric scraps, and probably not intended to outlast the following week. The intriguing small black doll (left) is made on an old-fashioned wooden clothing peg, and wears long underpants underneath to hide her 'legs'. She was designed to dangle from a thread, perhaps as a cot or pram toy to amuse a baby.

A brown-skinned cloth doll with moveable arms and legs was probably made from a kitset sold throughout New Zealand as a way for women to earn pin money at home. These dolls came in both 'black' and European colours. I have a box full of body parts and faces for them, along with the kitset instructions one woman bought in the '50s. Her efforts to make them were a failure, as her tetchy correspondence with the manufacturer details. I remember such dolls, with floral fabric bodies, being on sale in a stationer's shop in Masterton when I was a child.

Selection of homemade golliwogs, 1950s.

My mother's late 1940s copy of *Gifts You Can Make Yourself* includes a pattern for a black mammy nightdress case, and most craft publications, and pattern books for toys and bazaar items, seem to have included a golliwog in some form, such as a 1957 *Needlework* magazine, which calls a knitted black doll 'Honey-Chile — with all the wide-eyed piccaninnies' charm'.

I have never found such patterns for Maori dolls, though a knitted brown doll with blue eyes may have been intended to be one, as may a rag doll with a brown cloth body. It could be that this lack of Maori imagery suggests more sensitivity to Maori in this country at that time, at least in comparison with Australia, and a reluctance to stereotype them in the same way other racial groups — notably the Chinese — might have been.

Perhaps the most intriguing of all the dolls dealing with black culture that were made in New Zealand are 'topsy-turvy' rag dolls with a head on each end of a single body, one of which is obscured by a skirt until it is lifted and reversed. These dolls have a 'black' and a 'white' end, inviting the obvious question of which is supposed to be the 'right' one. Little girls found them delightful in part because the process of lifting their skirts seemed to be 'naughty'.

The tradition of these dolls dates back to 19th-century America, perhaps to the Civil War period, and possibly to Southern plantation nurseries. There is a theory they were made for black children who desired a forbidden white doll, but they are also known to have originally featured characters from fairy tales and nursery rhymes. A variation known as the Pennsylvanian hex doll, now in an American museum, has both a human and a pig head, and was used in the 18th century for casting spells and curing warts.

The 'white' dolls are invariably more worn than their black counterparts. Perhaps they were more popular with little girls.

LEFT: **Black man rag or duster bag, 1930s.**

RIGHT: **Black lady rag or duster bag, 1930s.**

five

Part Five: Taming the world

Images of Maori

LEFT: **Embroidered tea-cosy cover, probably 1940s. Designed to slip over a padded inner.**

If the world of black culture seemed far from New Zealand life, Maori were not. They may have had quite a distinct, separate status in the minds of European New Zealanders who had dealings with them, and with whom there was a good deal of intermarriage, but as the 1930s began, there was evidence also of a distinct Maori world in which different beliefs — religious and otherwise — prevailed from those of the European population. One measure of that was in declared religious beliefs.

Maori religious affiliation had been noted for the first time in the 1926 census, and while most described themselves as belonging to mainstream Christian churches, a great many Maori identified with those which were not seen as such by Europeans.

Of 65,693 Maori and 'half caste' in the population, in 1926, 11,567 were Ratana, 4540 Ringatu, 3804 Methodist 'Mihinare', 375 followers of Te Whiti and Tohu, 90 called themselves Maori Church, and 71 identified with the Seven Rules of Jehovah. Combined Maori and Mormon churchgoers numbered 23,908; mainstream Christians and the few Seventh Day Adventists among Maori numbered 35,084.

By the end of the '50s, some of these Maori religions had vanished from that table of religious professions; Ratana and Ringatu survived. Maori had also begun moving from their tribal areas into towns and cities. They were slowly becoming more visible to Europeans, but they barely featured in domestic textile handcrafts. For people like my parents, who

The Maoris are the most intelligent and cultured race of natives in the world. When young, the Maoris are beautiful, with rich brown skin, thick black hair falling over the shoulders, soft dark eyes, and sweet musical voices with a natural gift for poetry. They mature young, and after thirty lose much of their charm and become fat and often gross. This does not seem to trouble them, however, as they do nothing to check it . . . Maori princesses who are highly cultured, and educated in European ways, are sometimes taken as brides by men in high position and accepted by Society. It is not looked at with such favour, however, if a Maori courts a white girl, though now and again it is done and the marriage turns out often very happily . . . The instinctive courtesy and never-failing good manners of the Maoris no doubt help them to avoid many difficulties that ordinarily beset people who marry those of another race.

'THE NEW ZEALAND WOMAN AT HOME' BY M. WINIFRED GUY, WOMAN'S MAGAZINE ANNUAL, 1934

honeymooned in Rotorua in 1947, Maori were a tourist destination, or perhaps seasonal farm workers. Their world was not integrated into the imagery we chose, which resolutely harked back to Britain, and on the relatively few occasions when Maori imagery was used, it was integrated in such a way that its significance was altered and domesticated. One example of that can be found in Edith Howes' *Maoriland Fairy Tales*. In my Aunt Barbara's 1939 edition, the illustrations show the characters in the traditional stories as mostly pink-skinned and European-looking. The fairy wings, like angel's wings, which were common in European books of this kind sit oddly on a Maori figure draped in a cloth toga, and would have been a startling discovery in the New Zealand bush. Even the bush, in these illustrations, seems to be a whimsical botanical garden somewhere in Europe.

Within my family, I never heard overtly racist allusions to Maori, though Maori who lived the cottage idyll, as we saw it, rated greatest approval. Maori were judged, as everyone was by my family, in terms of their evident work ethic, the state of their houses, and the neatness and productivity of their gardens. My mother worked a season as a tobacco picker when I was a baby, and picked up some words of Maori vocabulary at that time. When I was a small child we used to stay some weekends with a Maori family in Pahiatua, and there were Maori children in my class at primary school. After I went to boarding school in 1958, however, I never again had a Maori in the same class at school, and I suspect that was not unusual for city-dwelling Europeans.

Statistics for Maori were kept separately during these three decades, on the basis both that the standard of record-keeping was too poor to be reliable, and that Maori were too physically isolated for data-keeping to be feasible anyway. Tucked away in a separate section in the official yearbook, it must have been easy to ignore the mute messages of their statistics. At the end of the '50s, the yearbook reports that most Maori were still living in country districts.

Embroidered doilies, 1940s–50s.

Detail of embroidered apron, probably 1940s–50s.

The birth rate for Maori, by then, was almost twice the European rate; Maori marriage records were erratic; the death rate was the lowest ever recorded for Maoris, and was in fact lower than that for Europeans in 1959. European men were living 14.24 years longer than Maori men; European women were living 16.55 years longer than Maori women; just over 3 per cent of the Maori population was aged over 60, compared with 13 per cent of non-Maori.

At the end of the '50s, Maori children were dying at three times the rate of Europeans, mainly from epidemic diseases as well as tuberculosis, respiratory and diarrhoeal diseases. In the period 1926–37, Maori babies had died at roughly the same rate as babies in Estonia, Uruguay and Latvia.

Yearbooks from this period are concerned with the degree of Maori blood being recorded in the population. This doubtless reflected the belief that Maori and Europeans would slowly assimilate over time through intermarriage. Then there would be no need for separate statistics at all.

The vast majority of Maori lived in the Auckland district in 1936 — 63,000 of them, out of 83,417 altogether in the North Island. In Hawke's Bay there were 6600; in Taranaki 4500; and in Wellington 9300. 'In the South Island Maoris do not attain any numerical significance,' the *New Zealand Official Yearbook* remarks, recording none.

It must have been easy for South Islanders, and the vast majority of people south of Auckland, to be truly unaware of Maori in the course of their everyday lives. They certainly do not seem to have been a source of embroidery ideas, though there were embroidery kits with New Zealand themes that women could buy, perhaps at tourist destinations. The few worked images of this kind that I have found are an interesting record of how European women stamped their own vision of the domestic idyll on Maori.

A Maori meeting-house tea cosy (shown on page 192), worked from a commercial pattern, features a Maori man of rank, and three traditional carved figures. It somehow manages to suggest the cottage shape of more traditional cosies, and would have had pride of place on the tea table just as a cottage cosy would have.

Consisting of two large and several smaller islands, the Dominion of New Zealand lies in the South Pacific Ocean some 1200 miles to the eastward of Australia. With South America some 6000 miles distant to the east and the Antarctic Continent 1600 miles distant to the south, the Islands are, for their size, among the world's most isolated.

THE NEW ZEALAND OFFICIAL YEARBOOK, 1940

RIGHT: **Embroidered tea cloth, probably 1950s, from the collection of Lauren Lysaght.**

A large doily also features a dwelling house, and a carved gateway (page 195). Beside the house stands a tree which is probably intended to be a ponga, although it looks rather like the palm trees in my mother's Mexican-themed embroideries of the '40s. In the foreground of these Maori images, traditionally worked cottage flowers are dotted, as if to prettify and tame their strangeness, or explain them to the viewer, and in a smaller doily there is a fence at the approach to a similar building which makes it look strangely suburban. A tray cloth lettered with the Maori greeting 'Kia Ora' is bordered with exotic imaginary flowers, and the cheerful images of tiki adapted to be almost like kewpie dolls. Another large doily features two young Maori women in traditional cloaks, one carrying a baby on her back; an identical doily is in Te Papa's collection. The figures look vaguely American Indian, and it's possible all these designs originated with commercial designers outside New Zealand.

A hand-worked linen tea cloth (right) is an exception; it seems to be entirely original in concept and execution, and it seems likely it was made by a Maori woman, as its imagery all relates to the Maori world. This cloth is a kind of mirror image of the handwork European women were doing at the time, but more personal, as if the maker had consciously decided to make a tea cloth with symbolism that had meaning for her, rather than the designs which were commercially available.

It is not possible to date the cloth, which was found in a thrift shop, but it fits into the tradition of the '30s through to the '50s, when women were working cloths like it in infinite variety. It depicts the North Island, Te Ika a Maui, divided into Maori tribal areas and with those areas, mountain ranges, volcanoes, lakes, islands and rivers delineated in pen and ink as well as thread. Maori formally define themselves in relation to rivers and mountains as well as their tribal groups and ancestors, references to all of which are made in the cloth.

Te Ika a Maui

Details from embroidered tea cloth, previous page.

The design includes a stylised canoe, lettered with the names of the seven canoes from which Maori tribes traditionally claimed descent, and decorated according to custom with representations of leaves and albatross feathers. The view of migratory history reflected in the cloth changed in the 1970s, when it was agreed there had probably been many canoes arriving here over time, not just one great migration, so the cloth certainly predates that change. Compass points are noted for north, south, east and west.

It is tempting to wonder whether the maker may have been Ngati Kahungunu, as that tribal area's lettering is bolder and larger than the others.

Each embroidered motif on the cloth has been selected for its cultural significance, almost in imitation of printed souvenir cloths, but more tightly focused on what is significant for Maori, rather than what is merely decorative.

The emphasis of the imagery is feminine and domestic in orientation, much as European women's work of this kind was at the time. The whare puni was a family dwelling or sleeping house, and the pataka a storehouse for food. Taro and kumara were cultivated for food in pre-European times, and the karaka berry was also a food supply. The tuna heke, or eel, was traditional food; its image is placed knowledgably on the side of the North Island where eel were known by Maori to migrate.

Hina pouri is the moon, and te puanga the evening star; rakau nui is the full moon. Both moon and star would have been significant in traditional cultivation of food crops, and the cycles of the moon were also significant for Maori weavers. Harakeke, or flax, was used for weaving, and also for medicinal purposes. Raupo was also used for weaving, and for making dwellings. The pukeko was a food source, and its feathers were used for cloaks.

The greenstone tiki was an important cultural icon, traditionally handed down from mother to daughter. Mere mere is a former term for a greenstone patu, or club, and the other traditional weapon depicted accurately here as a patu would have been carved from whalebone. Although the huia was long extinct when this cloth was embroidered, its feathers were still a symbol of rank and chieftanship. The kiwi was eaten by Maori, and its feathers used for cloaks. A teko teko is usually an ancestor figure. It is interesting that the sun is depicted with its rays hitting Mt Hikurangi on the East Coast, where dawn is said to break first in the world each day.

This unique cloth was a complex statement of cultural identity for its maker and her family. Simple stitches are used on it to great effect, and important detail is carefully delineated. It is the only example I have seen of what appears to be a Maori woman of this period using the European tradition to make a considered statement of her own in the language of thread. It's as if she looked at the European embroidery of women she knew, and felt compelled to record her response to it.

Images of New Zealand

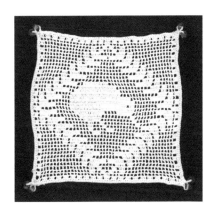

As embroidery is the art of the people, by which is expressed some idea, why not use what is here under your hand? People in New Zealand should think of their flora, their bush plants, mosses and many other things which are connected with the land they live in and love.

'EMBROIDERY A LIVING ART' BY LOUISE HENDERSON, *ART IN NEW ZEALAND*, SEPTEMBER 1941

LEFT: **Canterbury Centennial tea towel with deep crochet edging which has transformed it into a small tea cloth, 1950s.**

ABOVE: **Crocheted sugar-bowl cover with kiwi and fern imagery.**

Embroidery does not tend to do vistas well; it is about intimacy of scale. A woman at this time might embroider flowers, gardens, cottages, but she would not attempt to capture the real New Zealand landscape with any enthusiasm. It did not conform, in any case, to the images she had before her in embroidery books; the flowers and birds were all wrong. Fortunately, colonists had brought both with them from England, and a woman living in Auckland could write home about her cottage garden in the '30s, seeing and hearing only introduced birds. The clearing of land once covered in bush had destroyed many native birds which had driven early colonists mad with their unfamiliar song. Introduced species thrived, however, just as English colonists had done.

The sunshine is brilliant and very warm. And you should hear the birds! They begin singing in May and will continue right through the winter and spring. Thrushes, blackbirds, grey warblers, starlings, and a host of other birds too numerous to mention here, all pay their daily call to the bird-table. Thrushes and blackbirds are the chief songsters who, from dawn to dusk, fill our garden with sweetest melody . . .

LETTER FROM 'M.T.' TO 'AROUND THE EDITOR'S TEA TABLE', WOMAN'S MAGAZINE ANNUAL, 1937

RIGHT: **Detail of embroidered calico apron, probably 1940s.**

In 1950 Cantabrians celebrated the arrival of the first four ships there a century before. An Irish linen tea towel produced for the centennial celebrations is a comment on how colonists still saw themselves. The four ships are illustrated, and in the centre of the cloth is an idealised immigrant family. There are images of wheat, a campfire with a billy boiling above it, a sheep, a cow — and one image of an obviously native bird, a kiwi, which in this context looks oddly like a game bird suitable for eating. The cloth has a deep crocheted border, similar to crochet work of the previous century which would, however, have been white at that time.

The humble tea towel is telling about how we saw ourselves in 1950. We had been in Canterbury for a century; the first immigrants could possibly still be remembered by their living descendants, one of whom may have done the crochet. Our triumph was not how we adapted to what we found, but rather, how we adapted what we found to ourselves. We had made farms, the cloth tells us. We had made the landscape conform to the use of the countries we'd come from, and after a hundred years,

we could feel we were making history happen. There had been nothing but a vacuum before our arrival, it seems; there is no allusion to Maori.

Some native plants might find their way into cottage gardens at this time, but our main garden was the native bush. The landscape was spectacular, and still largely empty of people. Few tourists visited; there had been just under 8500 in 1930, and there were only 20,000 of them in 1959. I have found few images uniquely relating to New Zealand in domestic embroidery from this time.

I am not sure how much at ease New Zealand women were in the landscape, in any case. For many, it may well have been associated with isolation and loneliness. I know my Aunt Jean never walked more than a hundred yards from the McLeod homestead; although she lived on a large farm she did not care to explore the property, and seems to have mostly chosen to remain within the house, listening to classical music.

New Zealand literature at this time was concerned with the forming of a national identity, and examining the landscape symbolically. It was a landscape in which men struggled, as in John Mulgan's benchmark New Zealand novel *Man Alone*, but in which women could do likewise. Mona Anderson's *A River Rules My Life*, and her other accounts of rural life, were bestsellers. She was part of a pioneer tradition that still resonated with pride among European New Zealand women.

Colonists struggled to make a noticeable mark. Those they did make were of such subtlety in the landscape that they could often only be detected by a trained eye; they did not cry out to be recorded in needlework. There were no indigenous cuddly animals for women to take to their hearts, and translate into toys and embroidery, like the koala in Australia. The obvious decorative potential of kowhai, rata and native clematis seem not to have appealed at least until after the 1940 centennial, and the bush was a study in shades of green, an unpromising, limited palette.

Some kitset embroideries of scenic vistas from this era can be found in junk shops. An example is one of Mitre Peak in Milford Sound.

These embroideries always seem to have been executed in black or dark brown thread, and in the most basic of stitches, as souvenirs which crudely mimic magazine illustrations or etchings.

A doily which may be from a slightly later period — it is partly machine embroidered — seems to be an imaginary view of the Volcanic Plateau, and possibly two of its volcanoes, in stylised form. Typically its foreground, a Maori home and a storehouse structure, is the point of interest, and they are 'prettified' with incongruous dainty introduced cottage plants of a type which in reality could not thrive in that difficult volcanic soil.

An embroidered calico apron (see previous page), made from a commercial kitset, features a kiwi, mountains and a lake, with a tree fern, ferns and native flaxes. It is perhaps a sign of the desperate eye of the embroi-derer, looking for colour in this landscape, that the flax flowers are inaccurately coloured bright red. As with a landscape doily, there is the suggestion of a fence, with its obvious inference of domesticating Nature, and dividing it into manageable chunks.

One piece of embroidery on linen I have found does appear to be an attempt, in part, to depict New Zealand native bush. At the centre of this composition is yet another tree fern, or ponga, and beneath it some stylised tree shapes with yellow berries suggest they may be intended to represent karaka. The limited range of browns, greens and golds may be a concession to dominant colours of the bush, while the patterns formed by a range of embroidery stitches suggest gardens under cultivation rather than wilderness. This does not appear to have been worked from a kitset.

A linen tea cosy cover (right), which also seems to be an original composition, shows a beach scene with the figures of a woman, a little girl and a dog. The child is building a sand castle, and in the distance there is a row of small, red-roofed buildings. The clothing of the figures suggests it dates from the late 1920s or '30s. The emptiness of the landscape and sea, and the red roofs of the houses, suggest New Zealand, with its traditional roofs of painted corrugated iron. This embroidery seems to be one of the few that are not based on a purchased transfer; it displays a number of skilful embroidery effects and a variety of stitches. This is the only example I have found of a design featuring a woman and child together.

A doily from this period features a horse's head, and a distant house with a spire of smoke, snugly set into low hills and trees. In the foreground are coloured aster-like flowers. The scene could be anywhere in the world at that time, and the benign figure of the horse seems to represent tamed nature just as the hint of garden plants does. Nature was surely better tamed than terrifying to a colonist's eye.

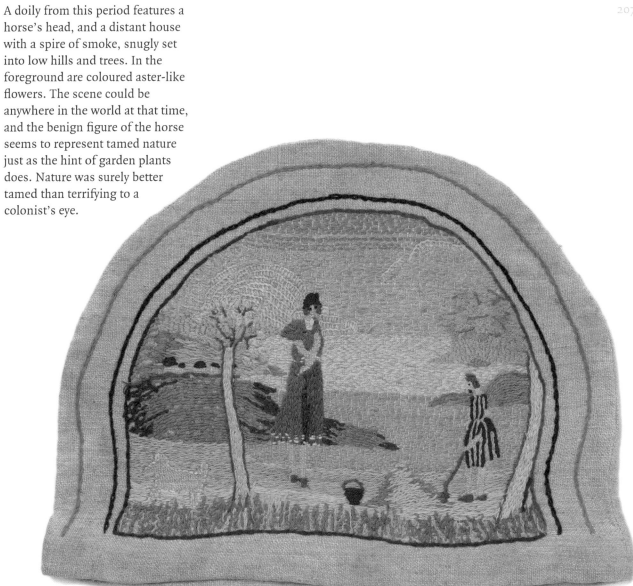

Embroidered tea-cosy cover, 1920s–30s.

Dolly Varden and her Kiwi garden

LEFT: **Dressing-table doily, 1930s.**

ABOVE: **Dolly Varden buttons, 1930s.**

At the present moment (June) our garden is fragrant with the scent of violets, daphne and luculia. Lemons and Poor Man oranges are ripening faster than we can use them. Arum lilies grow wild here, and are just beginning to bloom. In a month or so their stately whiteness will beautify many a neglected gully. Paper-white jonquils, too, are flowering in sheltered gardens.

LETTER FROM 'M.T.' TO 'AROUND THE EDITOR'S TEA TABLE', WOMAN'S MAGAZINE ANNUAL, 1937

Gardening, probably equally with embroidery, was a vital form of creative self-expression for New Zealand women from the '30s to the '50s. Like embroidery, its pleasures could be directly connected to a household's needs, and therefore justified. Women, confined to domestic life, beautified their homes with flower arrangements from their own gardens, and fed their families with the fruits and vegetables they grew. The garden was a vital foil for the cottage dream; inside and outside, a woman could construct her version of idyllic England.

If you were nothing more, primroses; than yellow and sweet,
I would ask Time to turn back again that youth and I might meet,
That I might go looking for you in a winding English lane,
And your tender fragrance so fresh in the mist, in the rain

I could not go on with my gardening
For dreaming of loved and lost London,
And Regent's Park on summer Saturdays . . .

MARY URSULA BETHELL,
COLLECTED POEMS, 1950

Like embroidery, gardening is a slow process; like embroidery, it is full of private challenges and triumphs. The tradition of flowers as a decorative theme in embroidery goes back centuries in Western culture, and women here continued to sew images of flowers and gardens that looked back to their countries of origin. In part, this must have been because their embroidery patterns and books mostly originated in England, though transfers were probably reprinted and possibly designed both here and in Australia. But it is also surely significant that they did not choose to devise their own imagery of native plants, preferring the loved cottage plants of the remembered English past, for most of the three decades. Native flowers did not seem to resonate with them, or to inspire the same emotions.

The gardens I knew as a child certainly did not feature native flowers, only the occasional 'kaka beak' shrub, or kowhai tree. I expect native plants would have seemed to be deficient in colour and smell; they lacked the sensuality expressed in the heady perfumes of the English cottage garden — heliotrope, roses, hyssop, flowering currants, wintersweet, daphne, orange blossom, lilac, pinks, violets. Besides, native flowers belonged in the bush, a chaotic world by comparison with the domestic garden.

My grandmother, in the 1920s, had planted the row of native trees, kowhai among them, that faced the road on her property, but that may have been a practical solution rather than an aesthetically driven one; native plants would be tough and withstand wind. She was a passionate gardener all her life, but all her struggles and triumphs were with introduced plants and vegetables. She grew a bed of fuchsias on the shady side of the house, hydrangeas, a huge magenta rhododendron, a grandiflora magnolia, oleander, camellias, and a maple. She grew English hybrid tea roses — the 1950s garden classics Queen Elizabeth, Peace and Ena Harkness among them. She grew bearded irises, dahlias, and scented spring bulbs that she paid astonishing sums of money for from plant catalogues.

Carpet felt tea cosies, 1930s.

Every spring she grew a planter full of bright mixed polyanthus at her back porch, and in autumn, without fail, she grew a border of bold African marigolds. There were larkspur, alyssum, verbena and geraniums. None of these garden plants, which gave her so much pleasure, was native to this country, but I doubt whether that thought ever occurred to her. Within the house she had arrangements of dried honesty seed pods, statice, goldenrod and yarrow for the winter. In summer she had rose bowls for her prized roses, and also for her huge gladioli blooms — this was a period in which flower arranging was a positive passion for many women, who strove to emulate English stylists like Constance Spry. The only native plant my family ever picked was toi toi from the roadside.

Gardens like Lucy's are typical of many in small-town New Zealand to this day; both a collection of personal memories and associations, and a homage to English cottage tradition. When my grandmother embroidered, she chose flowers from that tradition, or imaginary ones, and in this, too, she was typical of women of this time. Their embroidery was about the idea of gardens, rather than what they necessarily saw in front of them. They were not botanists.

A dressing-table set encapsulates the ideal garden of the '30s, as it featured in illustrated books, wall calendars, and women's magazines. Fan-shaped, each piece has an image of sundials set among paving stones, with hollyhocks, daisies and a rose bush. Birds fly above the scene in a tranquil sky. A more unusual large doily (shown on page 216) features dragonflies and water lilies, more symbols of peacefulness.

The garden is an idyllic place of rest, retreat and contemplation, embroideries tell us, the ultimate ordered world where flowers bloom in synchronicity under a blue sky. All it needs is a human being to appreciate it — and that human being was Dolly Varden, Sunbonnet Sue, or the Crinoline Lady. She seems to have been a person-ification of the ideal woman of the time, both decorative and decorous.

Dolly Varden's name is based on a character in the Charles Dickens' novel *Barnaby Rudge* who dressed in colourful and quaint costume. In embroidery she invariably wears a bonnet tied with ribbons, and is mostly depicted in profile. That is probably for stylistic reasons; it makes the bonnet's shape more attractive; but it also allows for how difficult it is to embroider a face convincingly, especially on a small scale.

This feminine figure is invariably seen in a garden setting, although, as with one embroidery transfer I have of her ironing, she may also be seen about the house, doing her housework. She is eternally youthful, and part of a range of images in which women depicted their lives as playful rather than grimly real. Sometimes she holds a posy of colourful flowers, rather like a young bride. Sometimes she

LEFT: **Dolly Varden embroidered apron, 1930s.**

ABOVE: **Embroidery transfer, 1930s–40s, incorporates two popular decorative motifs of the time, Dolly Varden and a Scotty dog.**

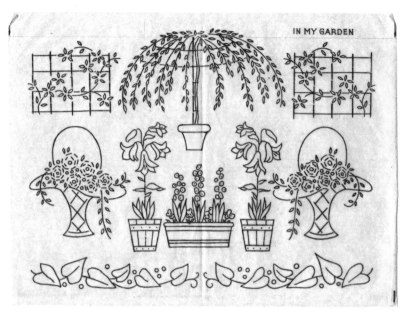

IN MY GARDEN

ABOVE: **Embroidery transfer motifs.**

RIGHT: **Embroidered tea cosy, 1930s, depicts an English-style herbaceous border.**

BELOW: **Embroidered handkerchief case, probably 1950s.**

holds a parasol. On one apron I have, (shown on page 212) she sits and reads on an outdoor sofa — inspirational verses, perhaps.

Dolly Varden's costume in part reflects fashionable dress at the time, in which versions of crinolines appeared for evening dress in both the '30s and the '50s — and women still wore hats, as she does, in their day-to-day lives. Like cottage flowers, the image of Dolly Varden was ubiquitous, a doll-like solitary figure whose origin may even relate to Christian art in which the Virgin Mary and female saints were seen with flowers.

Dolly Varden is most often seen with roses, delphiniums, hollyhocks and multicoloured aster-like daisies. In the language of flowers, as in Victorian nose-gays, which were coded messages, that suggests a confused state-ment. Hollyhocks — her most frequent companion — stand for female ambition; asters for love and daintiness; delphiniums, rather vaguely, mean 'airy'; and foxgloves suggest insincerity. I doubt, however, that New Zealand housewives meant much more by these flowers than that they made a pleasing visual arrangement.

A tea-cosy cover features a Dolly Varden in a wider and shorter skirt than usual, showing a tantalising glimpse of her lacy, long Victorian-style bloomers (page 149). A Dolly Varden on an apron wears a similar outfit, and carries a similar bouquet. A small, square doily has her sniffing flowers. These look suspiciously like pink rosebuds, in which case they would represent 'a heart innocent of love'. She stands on a crazy paving-stone path, similar to that in the dressing-table garden set of three doilies. And in another doily, which would have been part of a dressing-table set, her skirt is the inspiration for its scalloped shape. She features in miniature on the corner of a hand-kerchief and a large doily has Dolly standing under a blossom tree by flowers which suggest an English flower garden's herbaceous border.

A tea cloth and a further doily are both unusual in that Dolly's face is visible, along with her ringlets. The doily Dolly stretches out her hand toward a butterfly in an idyllic garden where once again, birds fly overhead. The four Dollys on the tea cloth's corners seem to be rather daringly holding out embroidered shawls behind them. The edge of this cloth is bordered in unusual multicoloured crochet. A sheer throw for a tea table or trolley has Dolly appliquéd in satin.

Dolly Varden is a figure who is tethered to the home, and the safety of the quarter-acre section. Her appeal for women must have been her link to the cottage idyll they strove to create. For 30 years she featured in embroidery designs, in book and magazine illustrations, in calendar pictures, and on greeting cards. She called women back to a remembered past which was by now a shared myth — and all she represented as a feminine ideal was about to be challenged and shattered in the decades to come.

Large embroidered doilies, 1930s–50s.

six

Part Six: Making do

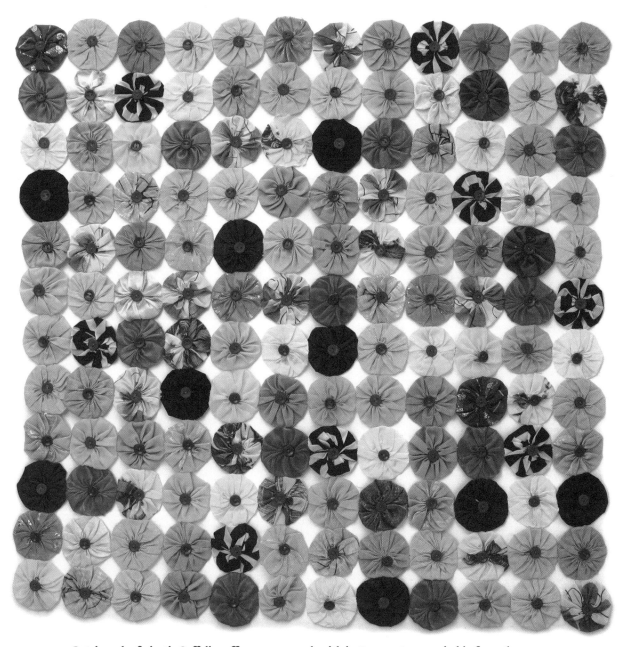

Patchwork of plastic Suffolk puffs or yo-yo work with button centres, probably from the 1950s.

Thrift and ingenuity

I grew up with thrift, my mother painting tins decoratively with leftover house paint to recycle them as storage canisters; never throwing away a cardboard box because they must always be useful one day; meals made from left-overs, and textile objects trimmed with scrap fabric. But these were only some of the many ways thrift — a highly valued virtue in my world — was expressed in every-day life.

It was a family legend how my great-grandmother Alice helped out a newly married son and his teenage wife by decorating their cottage with her own brand of thrift and ingenuity, thus setting them an example for the years ahead. There were not yet fireproof linings in wooden houses, and she carefully wallpapered their home with the shiny black-and-white pictorial centrefold sections of the *Weekly News*. This was one way of insulating their rooms from the wind, as well as making scrim-covered walls look fresh and clean.

Such wallpapering must have been common in 19th-century pioneer cottages, too; I saw it in the abandoned rabbiter's whare on the McLeod farm, where the frame of a cast-iron bed stood in a room papered with Victorian news-papers. But the newsprint there had yellowed; my great-grandmother's shiny paper would have stayed white for longer.

My grandmother talked about how people she knew improvised furniture during the Depression by turning wooden fruit boxes on their sides, stacking them, and stringing scrap fabric curtains across them for storage. My mother kept up that tradition in the 1950s when she painted the sides of a tea chest alternately dark red and white, and covered it with a homemade fringed tablecloth, and when she recycled a full '50s skirt printed with abstract ballet dancers as frills on my dressing table.

Because women worked with textiles they naturally turned to using them in thrifty and ingenious ways as a response to the need to economise. What impresses me is the careful way they made use of these fragments of cloth, making sure that attractive details of the pattern in even very small pieces were used to decorative advantage. If there was resentment at having to scrimp and save, pride at the result was still uppermost.

The most obvious and substantial of these fabric thrift and ingenuity projects were rag rugs and patchwork quilts, mainstays of cottage skills for a century here by this time, and still made in the traditional ways, though there was often carelessness in the execution. Maybe there always has been, and only the finest examples survive because they were so well made, and therefore always cherished. Then, too, some were probably never used because they were 'too good'.

Rag rugs typically used up worn-out woollen garments, which would prove long-lasting, and provide insulation in houses where people could not afford either conventional carpet or efficient heating. The garments — typically old coats and pullovers — were cut into strips, sorted for colour to create pictures or patterns, and painstakingly knotted through sacking until they formed a thick, patterned pile. It was possible to buy ready-made pieces of sacking, with a design already outlined for the maker to follow, during this period; I have one of them, unused, with a floral design.

Lighter cotton fabrics could also be used to create the pile, though they were less durable; I have a 1930s rug which must have been intended for a bedroom, where it would have relatively light wear; it is made from cut-up summer frocks.

Patchwork quilts came in handy for decorative purposes as well as for warmth. They were a means of recycling shirts, nightdresses and pyjamas, women's frocks and curtains of lighter weight. Some were made with patched woollen fabric or old blankets between the quilted top and a lining; others were throw-over bedspreads or tablecloths with only thin fabric backing, and I have seen patchwork illustrated in a contemporary magazine as curtains.

The tradition of making highly complex patchwork quilts, often featuring decorative needlework, luxurious fabrics and sophisticated quilting designs is centuries old. I have looked for simpler quilts from this period, those which are purpose-made by a woman of average sewing skill in response to need. Although some are quite crudely made, I see them as displaying an everyday, serendipitous creativity. Quilts such as these might have covered beds

on sun porches, holiday baches or spare rooms, effectively extra blankets in some cases; or the lighter ones may have been used as throws to cover worn upholstered furniture. However they must have worn out quickly if the furniture they covered was in constant use. I suspect that many were intended only as short-term solutions.

Among my quilts is one made from what seems to be woollen menswear fabric (right), possibly from drapers' samples or from cut-up leftover pieces of tailors' fabric pieced randomly together, and backed with samples of men's shirting. Such quilts were known as 'bush rugs' in Australia. The somber colour range of greys and blues is masculine and tasteful; I imagine it would have been used on a man or boy's bed, in the '20s or '30s. The idea of using fabric samples for patchwork like this is an old one; I have a 19th-century example, in colourful cottons. A small laundry bag I have is a variation on the idea; it uses the several colour ways of a manufacturer's samples of a 1950s floral design, sewn together in strips.

Patchwork quilt made from menswear fabric samples, probably 1930s.

Men make money but it is women who have to spend it. And women who usually have to save it — if they can. Can anyone save money these difficult days, and is it really worthwhile when its value always seems to be going down?

BRITANNIA AND EVE, JUNE 1956

BELOW: **Home-made handkerchiefs, 1930s–40s.**

RIGHT: **This golliwog and the set of silk remnant handkerchiefs were made by the same woman in the 1930s–40s. She also made plain handkerchiefs from worn-out white cotton sheets.**

A 1950s double-sided quilt of hand-pieced hexagons has a piece of woollen fabric as an inner lining to turn it into a useful blanket. An unlined quilt of large hexagons is crudely sewn with zig-zag stitch on a machine; women took to making these quilts on their sewing machines with more enthusiasm than skill, and as machines came to offer a range of stitches they exploited those possibilities rather than hand-stitching decoration as they had formerly done.

Patchwork was not just confined to bedding and throws. I have found a full-length 1950s crazy patchwork machine-stitched dressing gown (page 116); similar work, though much more detailed, and handworked, was done in Victorian times. A wartime copy of *Needlewoman* magazine refers back to that tradition, too, with its instructions for a patchwork evening jacket decorated with posies of flowers. I have a 1930s evening jacket worked in patch-work (page 225), as well as patchwork workbags and evening bags, aprons, and a tea cosy (page 146).

A favourite quilt of mine could be from the '60s, or even later, although it incorporates fabric scraps from '50s garments. I have tried to rescue it from total destruction by roughly stitching on harmonious pieces of fabric, because I wanted to preserve the unusual, mutinous embroidered wording of its maker. This crudely made 'crazy' patchwork quilt of rough and uneven-sized patches has an old grey woollen blanket sandwiched between its top and under sides. Wool blankets were scarce here in wartime, and this would have been one method of extending their usefulness.

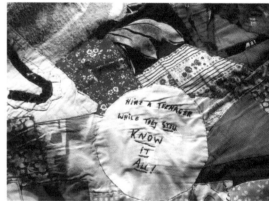

The embroidered written patches read: 'Insanity is inherited, you get it from your kids!', 'Hire a teenager while they still know it all!', 'Hard work never hurt anyone . . . but why take chances?', 'A woman's work is never done so why bother?' Embroidered initials on other patches must have had private significance for the maker and her family. It's interesting to see how a woman used needlework, so often thought of as a meek and submissive female pastime, to tease her family and rebel against domesticity — even as she practised it.

What exactly makes a home? One can think of many houses, beautiful in themselves and furnished with every comfort — even with luxury — which are yet only houses, comfortable abiding-places, but without the something which makes a home. On the other hand, I personally can remember when I was nursing on district — a room — one of many thousands, which was furnished with bare necessities, but contained an orange-box on which much loving care had been expended, transforming it into a little cot covered and frilled with cheap flowered muslin. Into this cot I presently put the newly arrived wee baby, and I can see the joy of it even now. The mummy and daddy were very young, and the daddy was out of work, but that room was a home!

NURSE SPICER, *WOMAN'S MAGAZINE
ANNUAL*, 1933

An unusual piece of patchwork, maybe intended as a small table-cloth for a side table, is made of assembled 'Sussex puffs' or yo-yo work pieces, each with a coloured button at its centre (shown on page 218). The fabric used appears to be samples of soft plastic shower curtaining or raincoat fabric that have been cleverly exploited for their strong colours and graphic appeal.

The appeal of patchwork for women surely moves beyond mere thrift and ingenuity into a kind of diary of their family and friends' curtains and clothing over time. The dressing gown, for example, is a blend of figurative, abstract and floral designs — there always seem to be roses and rosebuds — of satins and plain cottons, of lurex-threaded formal dress fabric, all in both modern and traditional styles, and covering possibly 20 years of women's fashion clothing. I suspect women shared their pool of fabric scraps around to achieve such variety.

I like the sense that there is a hidden jumble of memories in the pieces, and how patchwork of this kind creates cohesion out of so many disparate elements at a time

when there can't have been much non-conformist dressing; this was a society with tighter controls than we are now used to, and women were not encouraged to be rebellious. Maybe this was a subtle avenue for a desire to be different to tentatively reveal itself; patch-work is a kind of gentle tribute to chaos.

Women who made their own curtains were often left with offcuts of the material, and this was used in a great variety of ways. Some were predictably made into cushions, but curtain fabric also appears as aprons, tray cloths, place mats, dressing-table and tallboy mats, a dressing gown, a quilted tea cosy, and workbags. Some of this work must have been a legacy of wartime; furnishing fabric was not rationed, and women became adept at using it for clothing. That habit persisted into the '50s.

I have a homemade 1950s full-skirted sundress in mauve cotton; the maker has cut out flower shapes from curtain fabric and appliquéd them onto this backing. One small doily with handmade lace trim is made from a seamed piece of fabric that is obviously recycled; its main image is of a Dresden-style china figure of a man in the 18th-century dress that was so popular in '30s needlework. Other patched-together pieces of dress and curtain fabric have been used to trim and back oven mitts and oven cloths.

Women also crocheted and knitted wool rugs and cushion covers from scraps of colourful wool at this time, as they continue to do. Knitting wool was never thrown away. During World War II, it had been very scarce, as local mills had to give priority to military production. Some women gave up knitting then because wool was so hard to get, and the shortage continued into the 1950s. This explains my family's wool hoards, some of which would never be used; it may also explain the prevalence of striped and patterned woollen garments, which used scrap wool decoratively; I remember my mother finishing the front of a plain wool jumper she knitted me by breaking into rainbow stripes across the top section.

Patchwork evening jacket made from dressmaking scraps, 1930s.

My Aunt Barbara, a child of the Depression still, startled me in the 1980s by bringing me a suitcase full of old clothes which she expected me to cut down for my children. A 1930s needlecraft book suggests some ways of doing this; old knitted skirts, it says, can become knickers for schoolgirls; worn-out cotton frocks can be re-dyed and cut down to a child's size; adults' long woollen combinations can also become children's vests. Adult underpants can be scaled down to a smaller size, but you can't make children wear then.

A wartime copy of *Woman's World* suggests having your husband's suits remodelled while he's away at the war. A Melbourne tailoring firm advertises that they specialise in making over men's suits into tailored suits for women. It offers its own dressmaking patterns for recycling clothing, and advice on how to cut up an old damask tablecloth into serviettes, place mats and a luncheon cloth, crocheting the edges.

Sewing books of this period are full of detailed instructions for such exercises in ingenuity.

My mother surely drove herself quietly mad economising when she bought fabric; from growing up in the '30s she saw it as a challenge throughout her life to buy less than the pattern called for, so saving money, and had to juggle the pattern pieces around and adapt the garment accordingly. This was not always wholly successful.

Mending was an art that was practised routinely; I was taught to darn when I was a child in the '50s, just as my mother and grandmother had been before me, and my great-grandmother before them. Worn-out sheets were cut in half lengthwise and re-sewn with French seams to preserve the 'good' outside edges; I can remember how uncomfortable it was to sleep on the new seam. One magazine from this period takes this a step further, suggesting patterned fabric be added to the ends of sheets that have already been turned, so there is a decorative fold-back. Household linen was rationed in wartime.

My mother could 'turn' collars on shirts when they frayed along the neckline, reversing them so the unworn side of the collar was now uppermost. Woollen blankets were darned when they wore thin, and when they were too far gone, they were used as wadding between two sheets of patterned fabric, then stitched decoratively to make a padded quilt.

Stockings were mended, when they laddered, with nylon or silk thread that came in special hosiery-mending kits. Not only were stockings expensive, they were also in short supply at times. In 1938 silk stockings were one category of goods that were immediately affected as import restrictions intensified, and in wartime shortages were worse. However heavily darned a woman's stockings might be, they were still apparently better than naked legs — though it wasn't long before women's magazines suggested they might have to adjust to that idea.

RIGHT: **A black silk velvet and taffeta dress in my collection is an example of recommended recycling techniques; it uses these contrasting fabrics in a way that was often suggested for rejuvenating a tired or unfashionable garment.**

The dress is a 1940s length, but the fabric is suggestive of a decade earlier. The black silk velvet may well have begun life as a plainer (and longer) dress in the '30s which was then taken apart in wartime and reassembled with the floral pieces, perhaps recycled from another dress, or perhaps a cheaply bought remnant, decoratively patched in, and made into unusual decorative pockets. Diagrams suggesting ways to renovate old skirts were common, too; these invariably called for panels of contrasting fabric to be decoratively inserted in such a way, and a similar approach was used on sleeves and necklines. Women were invited to add contrasting sleeves in another fabric, or to reassemble a garment with an inserted panel of contrast in front. This dress ties in a bow at the back.

LEFT: **Most ingenious of the thrift toys in my collection is a doll from Alexandra in Central Otago. She seems to have been intended as a homemade replica of the sort of store-bought plastic doll that was popular in the '30s and '40s, and I suspect her face was physically moulded on one; its contours are similar. I imagine the woman who made the doll could not afford to buy the real thing from a shop, and had to improvise one for her daughter.**

The doll's face is made from fabric layered with many coats of flesh-coloured enamel paint until it was firm to the touch, with the features then painted on. The same care has not been taken with the painting of her flesh-coloured cloth arms and legs, suggesting the child she was made for could have asked for them to be painted to match at a later date; her torso is not coloured, and the original effect would have been like a doll from an earlier period; such dolls often had moulded, natural-coloured heads but plain calico bodies.

This doll's hair is made from sheep wool which looks as if it has been gathered from farm fences; she may be stuffed with more wool. She has a matching dress and bonnet, and felt strapped shoes and socks. Her fingers are stitched but not detached.

Women were especially ingenious at making toys. A golliwog from the 1930s on page 222 is dressed in soft striped silks which would have most likely been men's pyjama or shirting fabric, his outfit trimmed with women's dress fabric and Art Deco-style plastic buttons. His eyes are small mother-of-pearl buttons. The same maker sewed handkerchiefs from the striped silk, and from her old white sheets. The teddy bear on page 154 is made from soft woollen coat or dress fabric.

Holey socks and other knitwear were automatically darned to extend their lives, and so was anything at all that could be mended with needle and thread. Some patching was ingenious and complicated, like the mended section of an appliqué-work silk bedcover I have. Women's sewing books explained how to tackle such challenging exercises.

Throughout the 1930s and '40s, women's magazines recommended ways in which they could recycle old dresses and coats when they could not afford to buy new ones, sometimes by turning them inside out and re-sewing them with the fresher-looking side of the fabric outward. During the Depression many women could not afford to buy new material, and in wartime fabric was scarce even if they could; many items of vintage clothing show traces of remodelling.

Some of the thrift and ingenuity practised in my own childhood hung over into my own life as I grew up, and continues out of habit, making me a kind of grandchild of the Depression whether I like it or not. I still remove interesting buttons from clothes that have worn out, or which I send away for recycling — my mother would have kept zips and buckles as well — though I will most likely never use them. I have made children's clothes which would have been cheaper to buy, and I've mended them when it would have made more sense to replace them.

I have been known to mend laddered pantyhose, and I darn knitwear if I'm fond of it. I recycle suitable soft fabrics when garments wear out, to use as rags and polishing cloths. I change my clothes at home to save wear on 'good' clothes, and have been guilty of saving clothes 'for best' for so long that they've hardly ever been worn when they are no longer remotely fashionable. All of this would have been considered very sensible, even obligatory, by my family, and most of them strike me as faintly absurd even as I keep up habits ingrained into me by their example. Practising such economies has become a kind of ritual, and I don't expect they will reach into my own children's lives. That's how long it has taken one family to recover from war and Depression — and I never lived through either. My legacy, from my mother and my grandmother, is a kind of false memory.

Do not discard an old coat and skirt. With a little thought and manipulation it will make a very warm winter dress. The coat will overlap the skirt and give scope for an interestingly shaped waist or hip join. The crossover, if any, can be used for good purpose too. Not very much can be done with the sleeves because there is seldom much spare material; they could be shortened in a shaped line and patterned material used for the lower part of the sleeve. The skirt may have to remain very much as it is. A wrapover can be turned into a pleat or, if there are enough cuttings to make them, pleats can be let into an existing seam.

THE PICTORIAL GUIDE TO MODERN HOME
NEEDLECRAFT, EDITED BY CATHERINE
FRANKS, 1943 EDITION

Handkerchief sachet made from fabric fragments, probably from the 1930s.

Unfinished wool hearth rug, probably 1920s or '30s.

The sugar-bag years

A **popular history** of New Zealand in the 1930s is called *The Sugarbag Years*, in reference to a time when even the most unpromising materials had to prove useful. Women displayed great ingenuity in the uses they found for old sacking sugar bags at this time, and continued that tradition well into the 1950s.

There was little inhibition shown about displaying the stamped insignia of the Colonial Sugar Refinery; perhaps with some women it was a matter of pride to show their thriftiness frankly, especially with heavy-duty items like oven cloths which were bound to become stained and scorched. But most women seem to have kept the insignia on the side of the object that was less visible, in an attempt to help prettify the most mundane and rough fabric they would ever sew.

Oven cloths appliquéd or patch-worked with sewing fabric scraps, or embroidered with wool, were probably the most universal sugar-bag pieces in New Zealand homes. Sacking laundry aprons were also popular; women had to keep a fire going underneath their copper on wash day, and sacking aprons were more practical for the hard work involved in laundering without a machine than their usual fabric ones.

RIGHT: **Embroidered sacking workbag, 1930s–40s. Dress fabric lining.**

FAR RIGHT: **Detail of embroidered sacking workbag, 1930s–40s.**

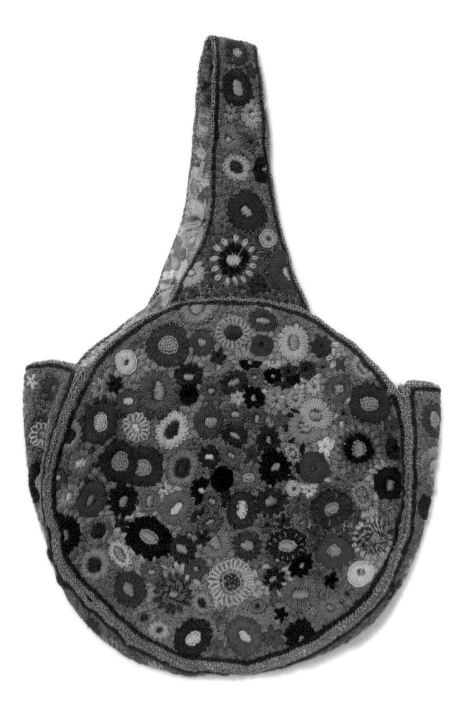

These sacking aprons, which were probably used for other hard and dirty work around the house and garden, display a good deal of impromptu creativity. I am especially fond of a box-pleated apron (left) trimmed with dress fabric that reflects the tailored look of fashionable clothes in the 1940s. It seems to be an ironic reference to the impossible dream of high-fashion glamour while performing rough household tasks.

My most basic Depression sacking apron is merely a basic shape trimmed with floral scrap fabric around its edges. Others are appliquéd decoratively but crudely with dressmaking trimmings, or embroidered with large wool flowers (page 250).

A sacking rag or laundry bag is made into an improvised doll with a padded face and feet, and a '50s sacking oven cloth is elaborately patchworked with many tiny squares of patterned material, a technical showpiece the maker evidently could not bring herself to use. The crudest nightdress case I have seen is made from an envelope of sacking crudely appliquéd with scraps of Depression-era floral curtain fabric, and a '50s peg bag of duffel-bag shape is embroidered with woollen flowers and lined with dress fabric.

The most dramatic pieces of sacking work are probably the 'black people' rag bags which women made in the '30s. Like the golliwogs housewives busily made for their children in this period, these black figures gave their makers creative licence to indulge in bold strokes of colour and whimsy, and objects like them must have held cheerful pride of place on many washhouse walls. There was not yet an awareness that such images could be seen as racist.

LEFT: **'Tailored' sacking apron made from sugar sacks, 1940s. The reverse side is stamped with the mark of the Chelsea Sugar Refinery.**

RIGHT: **Black lady rag bag with recycled dress fabric.**

The workbag

A workbag, and work to put in it, are essential during a country-house visit . . .

'COUNTRY HOUSE VISITS' BY NOMA CLARKE, *WOMAN'S JOURNAL*, JULY 1937

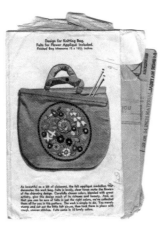

I never knew my mother not to have a homemade workbag hanging from the corner of one of her wooden framed easy chairs. It was a habit she'd picked up from her own mother and the other women in her family. Within the workbag would be her latest knitting or crochet project; something was always in the process of being made. A workbag would go out with her when she went visiting informally, and she would work at her project — usually knitting — while she talked. Otherwise her handwork was always near at hand at home in her workbag, ready for any spare moments.

LEFT: **Embroidered felt workbag, 1930s.**
ABOVE: **Workbag pattern, 1930s.**

Variety of appliqued felt workbags, 1930s.

Workbags in various styles and techniques, 1930s–40s.

The workbags of the '30s, '40s and '50s came in a huge variety of styles and shapes. They must have been popular; craft books and magazines of the time often include patterns for them. Some bags are plainly designed to accommodate knitting needles, which could fall out of bags with shallow sides; my mother had one zipped workbag she used exclusively for them. Some are made from remnants of furniture or dress fabric, but they seem to have been made with a wish to make them attractive and decorative even if they were only for home use. Others, I suspect, were intended for taking out when visiting, and so they serve as a way of exhibiting the maker's fashion sense and skill; they're a sort of best handbag equivalent, kept stored in a drawer most of the time.

The dominant category of 1930s workbags is felt; with graphic, coloured felt-appliqué designs. These designs are usually floral; the favourite flowers depicted on them are variations on those old cottage-garden favourites, hollyhocks and foxgloves. One unusual example in my collection has knitted appliqué flowers; some felt flowers were made in layers to give the impression of being similarly three-dimensional. Since a few styles in felt bags recur and are close to identical, though made in different colours, there may have been commercial patterns for them, though I have never found one.

Featherston antique dealer Campbell Moon remembers his aunt teaching Country Women's Institute members how to make them during his Wairarapa childhood in the late 1940s, when she taught him to make foxglove shapes in felt. Once they learned the basics, women were free to experiment with both embroidery and appliqué on the felt, an easy medium to work with, and forgiving of mistakes. A pattern for such a bag must have been barely necessary for a competent sewer, though I have discovered one '30s example (shown on page 238). This workbag is designed to be made from fabric, probably crash, a soft oatmeal-coloured hessian-like fabric with a loose weave, with a decorative panel of felt appliqué.

An outstanding larger workbag (second from right, above) is made from taffeta. It features multicoloured lazy daisies worked in chain stitch. Others were embroidered in wool on crash; women often painted wooden handles for these bags to complement the colours they stitched.

One bag is made from knitted string, embroidered in wool (third from left, above); it could be either a shopping bag or a workbag. I suspect this bag, which features an embroidered butterfly and flowers on one side, and a sprig of bright, stylised flowers on the reverse, was made by a Pacific Island woman.

It reminds me of primitive paintings I have seen by women from that ethnic back-ground, and is the only workbag-style bag I have discovered which seems to come from a decorative tradition to one side of the mainstream.

My mother's copy of *Gifts You Can Make Yourself* from the 1940s has a pattern for an apron workbag for keeping knitting in while working around the house. The principle is the same as for the one her grandmother wore at the end of the 19th century.

The apron

Just why several of the leading Paris fashion houses should have gone in for aprons this spring, is one of those mysteries that are never satisfactorily solved. Perhaps aprons are a part of the increased femininity of the mode in general, for no garment is more sweetly feminine than an apron.

'PARIS SUGGESTS AN APRON' BY MARY HAMILTON, GOOD HOUSEKEEPING, MAY 1939

LEFT: **1950s print apron.**

Aprons used to be a universal female uniform. To illustrate a man wearing an apron was a recognised joke; men did not perform household tasks, and only a henpecked husband would agree to put one on. But aprons were also complex garments which appeared in many guises depending on a woman's role on the day. She could be a fashion plate, a seductive minx, a drudge; she could express something about her personality and her attitude to her daily tasks even as she submitted to the role of housewife.

If women often had limited wardrobes during the '30s, '40s and '50s, they certainly did not lack for apron-wardrobe potential. There were aprons for every possible nuance of formality and informality, and for every type

of work; from playing at being a formal hostess to burning rubbish in the back yard. Fine embroidery skill might be lavished on them, or they might be just a crude sacking oblong bound with cloth; it could be like the difference between wearing a ball gown and wearing dungarees.

Most aprons seem to have been expressions of thrift; curtain and dress fabric remnants were often used, as were sugar bags. Especially small scraps of fabric were made into patchwork aprons, sometimes bound with scraps of lace trimming or braid, or used as appliqué.

Everyday aprons were usually cheerful cotton; some women preferred bib fronts for their greater coverage, especially if they were large people. Bright colours and patterns were accentuated with contrasting trims. Such aprons were easy to make, requiring only a little fabric, which could be cheap and cheerful; often the pattern had kitchen or food themes. I suspect many of these aprons were made as gifts for other women, as a way of using up leftover fabric from home dressmaking; magazines and craft books regularly published suggestions for new styles, and suggested they'd make ideal gifts. Many everyday aprons were made from curtain fabric; they would have been sturdy and strong.

For special occasions a woman would put on one of a variety of fancier aprons, designed to be frivolous and impractical, rather like party dresses. One craft book from the '40s suggests that a woman might like to have separate aprons for morning and afternoon, echoing the way fashionable women of the day changed their outfits several times a day. Printed cottons would be suitable for mornings, it suggests, and printed crepe de Chine for after lunch.

A fancy apron was an extreme style statement of a kind; such aprons were ruined if they were marked, just as best tablecloths were, and many — such as the heavily embroidered '30s examples, or crocheted aprons — must have taken hours to make. Their very impracticality suggested luxury.

LEFT, TOP: **Crocheted apron, 1930s.**

LEFT, BOTTOM: **Sun-ray style apron, 1940s.**

RIGHT: **Print bib-fronted wrap apron, made from rayon dress fabric, 1950s.**

It's clear that a decorative apron could have been a virtual fashion accessory in a domestic setting; it would have breathed new life into a stale wardrobe. Some aprons are in fact virtually dresses; these two examples from the 1930s have dummy decorative fronts and collars like smart street wear, only their open backs and fabric ties revealing their true purpose. Wearing garments like these, a housewife was protecting the real dress underneath, which in the Depression might well be quite threadbare; she also had the luxury of pretending she was dressed up. In fact, she might only have needed to wear an old petticoat underneath.

Such overall aprons are close relations of the house coat, or house dress, which was made solely for wearing at home while performing domestic duties. A '30s example I have has a full-length buttoned front opening, and pockets. Such garments saved wear on clothes needed for public appearances, but they could be quite glamorous in their own right. A woman did not need to be corseted when she was wearing them, which must have been a relief; bending and carrying heavy objects — children among them — can't have been easy for those who were so constrained.

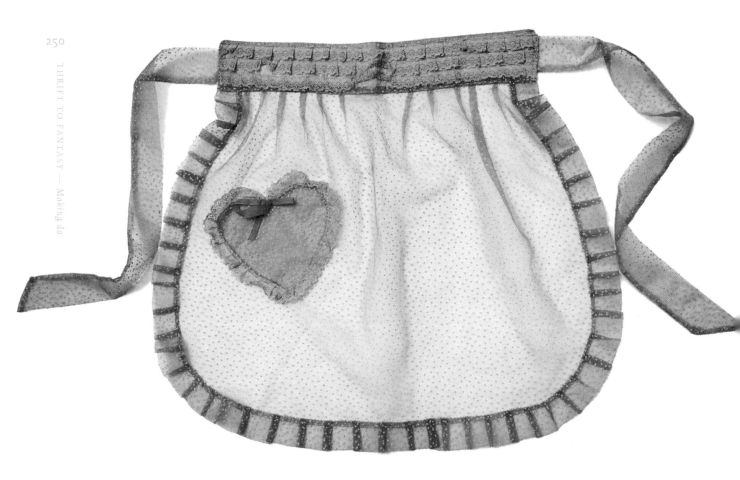

Most frivolous of all were the aprons made of sheer fabrics, supreme hostess aprons designed to float ethereally over the garment beneath, and offer almost no protection whatsoever. These could look almost flirtatious; a '50s flock nylon example looks perilously like racy lingerie (left).

The greatest contrast to these wafting bits of nonsense was the sacking aprons worn for heavy household work (right). Sacking, being loose-weave and cheap, is not made to last for ever, but even these aprons could be well designed and crafted. Those that were embroidered with wool were a concession to style even when chopping firewood or scrubbing the back porch with sand soap, as my grandmother regularly did.

Aprons were practical, but they were also an admission that a woman accepted a traditional role in the home. They said explicitly that a woman was a housewife at a time when that was in fact what most women were.

LEFT: **Sheer flock-nylon hostess apron, 1950s.**

RIGHT: **Embroidered sacking 'heavy duties' apron, probably 1940s–50s.**

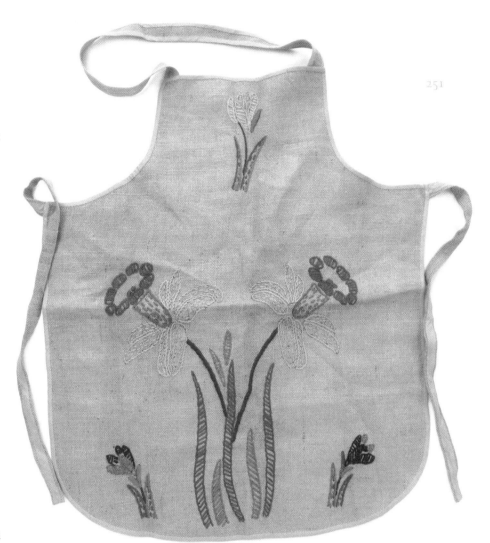

TAPESTRY 18

10¢ 6

QUALITY NEEDLES

Boye

MADE IN ENGLAND

THE BOYE NEEDLE CO.
CHICAGO

NEW YORK   SAN FRANCISCO

Wᴹ CROWLEY & SONS,
EXTRA PATENT FINE
POLISHED   CAST STEEL
CREWEL   6   EMBROIDERY
Made in   England

JOHN ENGLISH
& CO.
FECKENHAM, ENGLAND.
19¢
JOHN H. PRATT.
GEO. P. FARMER.
20
BETWEENS
8
MADE IN ENGLAND.

QUEEN VICTORIA
SILVER EYD
SHARPS
3/9
WARRANTED

H. MILWARD
& SONS'
PATENT HELIX
NEEDLES
MADE AT REDDITCH, ENGLAND.

SHARPS
2/0
PATENT WRAPPERS
J. F. MILWARD
SOLE AGENT
1857
REG. U.S. PAT. OFF.
25 NEEDLES

CLINTON
Quality   Notions

PINS   THIMBLES
SAFETY PINS   TIDY PINS
BUTTON PIN'EMS   HOOKS & EYES
VEIL & HAT PINS   SNAP FASTENERS

NEEDLES
(MADE IN ENGLAND)

SHEFFIELD STEEL
GREEN   OAK
NICKEL PLATED

15
SUPERIOR
QUALITY
NEEDLES

SHARPS 8

20
NEEDLES   10
CENTS
MILWARDS
NEEDLES
MADE IN ENGLAND

LARGE EYE NEEDLES

MADE IN ENGLAND

REG. U.S. PAT. OFF.

Crowley's
LION BRAND
NICKEL PLATED
CREWEL
EMBROIDERY
8
W. CROWLEY & SONS

Crowley's
LION BRAND
CREWEL
EMBROIDERY
5/10
15 NEEDLES

Wᴹ CROWLEY & SONS,
EXTRA PATENT FINE
POLISHED   CAST STEEL
CREWEL   6   EMBROIDERY
Made in   England

R.H. Macy & Co.
Inc.
Notion Department
Best English
NEEDLES
MILLINERS
5/10

H. MILWARD
& SONS
PATENT HELIX
NEEDLES

TAPESTRY
19 to 24
J. F. MILWARD
SOLE AGENT
1857
25 NEEDLES

MADE IN ENGLAND

WAR PACK

NEEDLES

Marshall
& Co.

SHARPS
3/9

EMBROIDERY
4/8

UNIVERSAL
10 NICKEL PLATED NEEDLES
5 CTS
MADE IN ENGLAND

Sewing things

Sewing may have been a universal necessity for women, but they found ways to personalise the accessories they used. Homemade pieces, and the tools that went with them, would have been in most New Zealand homes at this time: a fabric holder for knitting needles, a pincushion which is also a cotton-reel holder, a gathered 'handkerchief' style sewing bag for needle packets and small thread holders, assorted pincushions and needle holders, either embroidered or made from scrap fabric or felt. A china half-doll wearing a full skirt was made by my mother in the '50s; her skirts lift to reveal a pincushion base. Such half-dolls, with holes at their waists, could be purchased at chain stores in the '30s.

TOP: **Box of silk hosiery mending thread, 1930s.**

ABOVE: **Pincushion doubling as a cottonreel holder, made from furnishing fabric, 1950s.**

LEFT: **Variety of needle packets. Note, packet at bottom left is marked 'War Pack', from World War II.**

LEFT: **Needlework projects like this fold-out sewing kit were popular during this era. A scrap of a luxurious old brocade, probably left over from a piece of formal evening wear, has been used as the folding back for this one, secured shut when not in use with an ornamental metal button. It opens to reveal an interior in which blue taffeta is edged with rows of ornamental stitches, and a place has been made for items such as threads, embroidery scissors, pins, needles and thimble. Sections are neatly embroidered with foxgloves and bouquets of cottage-garden flowers.**

BELOW: **Small needleholder, probably 1950s.**

RIGHT, TOP: **Feltwork elephant pincushion with weighted base, probably 1930s.**

RIGHT, BOTTOM: **Opened book of embroidery threads, 1930s.**

Personal accessories and gifts

'It's thrilling to see something growing under your hands,' was a comment made by a young wife who was just being initiated into the craft of dressmaking.

THE BOOK OF GOOD HOUSEKEEPING, 1940S

There were few glamorous accessories for the women of the '30s, '40s and '50s to buy to cheer up their homemade outfits. The Depression, World War II and then import restrictions meant they had to struggle to express their desire for fashion and style, and a little glamour. Having made their own clothes, re-made them, recycled them into something different yet again, they were obliged, often, to make their own accessories and carry them with pride.

At a time when a woman might have only one tailored suit to her name, or two dresses and one coat, she had to rely on accessories to change the way they looked on different occasions. Scarves were popular for this reason, as were brooches, bangles and necklaces that became focal points of colour.

ABOVE: **Embroidered comb case, 1930s.**
RIGHT, TOP: **Handworked belt, 1940s.**

What could not be bought had to be made with the materials available, and women's magazines constantly rose to the challenge of providing inspiration.

Hats could be knitted, crocheted, remodelled endlessly using lengths of netting, homemade artificial flowers, and decorative homemade hat-pin tops made from felt. Handbags could be made from raffia, crochet or scrap fabric. Scarves were made from dressmaking leftovers, and so were handkerchiefs, which were then edged with tatting or crochet. Homemade scarves could be tucked into the neckline of a suit; women often wore nothing but underwear beneath them, but the scarves suggested there could be a whole blouse. Women also made false blouse fronts, designed to be visible when a jacket did not button up firmly, and to suggest a whole garment.

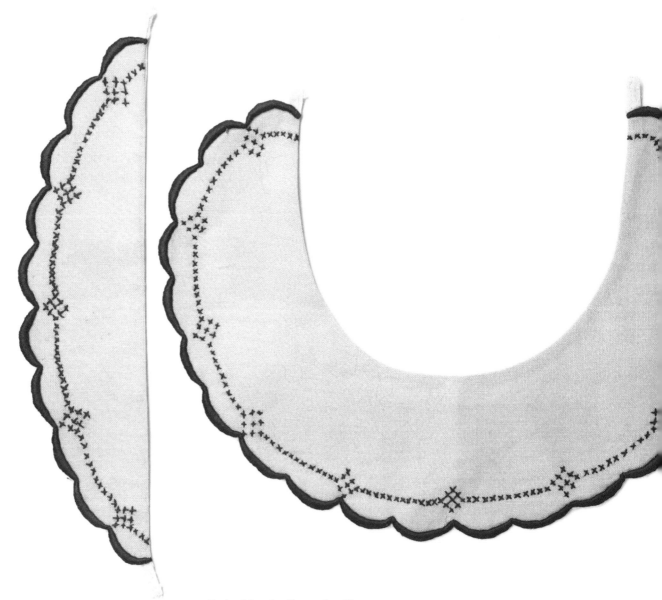

Embroidered collar and cuff set, 1930s.

The pride of the chef who said he could make a succulent meal out of a pair of kid gloves; that of the midinette who, in fashion, could rival the wife of a millionaire with a yard of chiffon and a flower. This pride may be ours today, but it means intelligence, knowledge, self-discipline, and that gift of the gods: a sense of humour.

'A NEW FLAVOUR — AND A GAY BRAVERY' BY MOMA CLARKE, WOMAN'S JOURNAL, DECEMBER 1939

Belts were another important fashion accessory in the '40s and '50s, drawing attention to a corseted slim waistline with a colourful plastic buckle or an interesting texture. Women wove or knotted them from string, tape and straw; I have a Dryad Handicrafts leaflet explaining how to do cord knotting; and they sometimes embroidered fabric belts as well.

Crocheted gloves, in these times when a properly dressed woman had to wear gloves when she went out, were a popular accessory, and many patterns were printed for them. My mother was among the many women who made them. Women also crocheted their own string bags for carrying shopping.

Beneath their outerwear, women made their own lingerie and nightdresses. I have a nightdress length which has been ready-packed in a shop in the 1940s with a picture of suggested styles for knickers, camisole and petticoat as well as nightdress — doubtless from a contemporary pattern book. Many women must have enjoyed the fine hand sewing involved, a hidden display of specialty skills like faggoting and French seams.

Another vital accessory was detachable collars for plain frocks, which could change their appearance from day to day, or even from day to evening wear. These were often crocheted, but they were also embroidered, sometimes with detachable cuffs to match (shown on page 258).

The most popular handbags for women to make were clutch purses which did not require special purchased parts like frames and handles. These seem to have been especially popular in the 1930s and '40s. I have a large black felt handbag of this kind from the '30s (see page 257), expertly over-stitched, with appliquéd flowers. A green felt clutch bag shuts with dome fasteners and is stiffened inside with a hard plastic lining beneath an attractive lining of printed dress fabric. It is embroidered with a brightly coloured bird sitting on a branch of a tree. Yet another homemade clutch purse has fabric flowers appliquéd and embroidered on it, with matching fabric trim. It shuts with a snap fastener and is decorated with a glass button-like trim. A ruched and pleated circular bag is made from floral crepe dress fabric; possibly it was made to match it. It closes with a zip fastener. A 1950s handbag features tapestry irises on a black ground. The execution of this bag hasn't been entirely successful; it may have been made to fit a recycled frame. An unfinished piece of needlepoint was intended to become an evening bag that would have been attached to purchased fittings and handle.

Women produced a wide range of gift accessories as presents for each other during these three decades. Covers for powder compacts and powder puffs were common, either crocheted, embroidered, or made from scraps of fabric, then tatted around the edge. A tube-shaped variation on this theme, sewn from a scrap of dress material, is made to cover a handbag-sized cylindrical container of powder. Face powder was a basic cosmetic, worn by all women when they went out.

Small shallow embroidered envelopes of fabric were intended to be comb covers (shown on page 256). Larger embroidered envelope-shaped bags were meant to hold slippers (shown on page 117). A pink crocheted set of buttons and a bow must have been a long-ago gift intended to cheer up the front of a blouse. A boxed felt necklace from Molly Bawn Products of Auckland, from the '40s, may well be an example of a woman hoping to branch out from making such gifts for her own friends and family, to earn some pin money. Such felt-work projects were popular in craft publications and women's magazines. The necklace would have sat over the top of a sweater with a high neckline. It ties at the back with a simple length of coloured cord.

By far the most popular gift items seem to have been handkerchiefs and handkerchief sachets; there was a virtual cult of the handkerchief. Especially pretty scraps of crepe de Chine, silks and georgettes were hemmed for use as handkerchiefs, and sometimes trimmed with lace or tatting edges. A woman might also embroider the corner of a purchased handkerchief as a way of personalising an inexpensive gift. Handkerchief sachets appear in a variety of shapes and styles, often embroidered, and displaying great ingenuity in their treatment.

Fashion photographs of this period often feature a decorative handkerchief protruding from a woman's tailored pocket, or held in an elegant hand. They were a small but important accessory for the well-dressed woman at a time when she was able to express her fashion sense most effectively through details.

A make-believe miniature 'shirt' handkerchief sachet seems to have been a popular gift. Mine has a typed inscription attached to it:

> If your handkerchief is dirty
> Put it in this little shirty
> And a new one you will find
> In the turned-up tail behind

Dirty handkerchiefs were obviously meant to be stored in the main part of the 'shirt', and clean ones in a separate section at the back. This seems an odd idea. Maybe it was intended for holding used expensive 'dress' handkerchiefs, too delicate and special to throw into the household's main wash.

Epilogue

The Family is a group of 35 cloth dolls made by Malcolm Harrison between 1983–1987, and purchased by the Dowse, Lower Hutt, for its collection. Each doll is named, and has its own brief story, here in Harrison's own words.

THE GROUP OF THREE (left to right): Lennox, Thomas and Bank. Lennox is Thomas's oldest son, who frightens Maia (another member of The Family) with frogs and worms whenever he can. He and his brother Bank are often in trouble. Thomas is a champion swimmer, oarsman, runner and horse-rider. He doesn't care much for a normal lifestyle and is now working at a circus sideshow. Bank is a total terror. He is always finding frogs and worms, and those he doesn't give to his older brother he mixes in the baking.

THE COUPLE: Cassandra-Edith and Emerston. Emerston's latest show-girlfriend, Cassandra-Edith, has quite a number of plans for herself and Emerston. She has started them by becoming a friend of Victoria (another Family member).

Looking back on the textile traditions of these three decades, culminating in the 1950s, there is no hint of a growing alternative to the buttoned-down world of domestic New Zealand. In the background, though, there were warning signs of what was to come. In 1950s cinema, rebel figures like James Dean and Brigitte Bardot found a receptive young audience; Jackson Pollock's splatter paintings celebrated a new, and unrecog-nisable style of modern art; beatniks in black sunglasses might have been seen in dark side streets of Wellington and Auckland; as well as New York and London. We may have been governed by the farmers' party, a royal visit may have been exciting, afternoon-tea parties continued in small towns, but a change would come in the '60s and crafts would soon be a half-forgotten tradition associated mainly with older women.

**Thrift and ingenuity themes
from the past inspired these
felt handbags by Vita Cochran,
which incorporate recycled
buttons and zips.**

ABOVE: **What appears to be a traditional tea cosy is in fact a knitted evening bag by Vita Cochran, complete with a compartment to hold a cell phone.**

RIGHT: **Detail of felt bags by Vita Cochran.**

ABOVE: **Felt flowers echo the craft bags of the 1930s.**

BELOW: **Cochran's French poodle is a reminder of the popularity of these dogs as a decorative motif in the 1950s.**

Yet these crafts did not die out altogether. Time passed, perhaps they lost their association with conservatism, and they are being re-interpreted and redeveloped for a new audience. Artist Lauren Lysaght works with ideas that link to past craft traditions. Fellow artist Malcolm Harrison trained first as a dressmaker, but became an innovative embroiderer and textile artist whose work is sold in art galleries. He donated his 'family' to the Dowse, a group of cloth dolls made within the craft and golliwog tradition, incorporating and reinterpreting textile fragments (page 262). Dunedin craftswoman Vita Cochran has art-history training, but comes from a family which has always practised traditional textile crafts. She has been inspired by crafts to make creative handbags and accessories, working with fashion designer Marilyn Sainty to give them contemporary relevance.

Bibliography

Armes, A c1930, *English Smocks*, The Dryad Press.

Australian Home Budget (1926–49) *Toys, Novelties, How to Make Them in Crochet, Knitting, Fabric etc.*, Australian Business Services.

Barnett, S 1993, *Those Were The Days: 1930s*, Moa Beckett.

Belich, J 2001, *Paradise Reforged*, Allen Lane The Penguin Press.

Cook, O and Smith, E 1954, *English Cottages and Farmhouses*, Thames and Hudson.

Crawford, M 1952, *Queen Elizabeth II*, George Newnes Ltd.

Crawford, M 1953, *Happy and Glorious!* George Newnes Ltd.

Dann, C 1990, *Cottage Gardening in New Zealand*, Allen & Unwin.

Department of Education 1982, *The Home Front: Life in New Zealand During World War II*, Wellington.

Dymock, G 1990, *Good Morning New Zealand*, Moa Publications.

Ebbett, E 1981, *Victoria's Daughters*, Reed.

Ebbett, E 1984, *When the Boys Were Away*, Reed.

Fitz Gerald, P 2003, *Warm Heritage*, David Bateman.

Fry, G W 1943, *Embroidery & Needlework*, Sir Isaac Pitman & Sons Ltd.

Gifts You Can Make Yourself 1947, Odhams Press.

Isaacs, J 1997, *The Gentle Arts*, Lansdowne.

Jekyll, G and Jones, S R 1944–45, *Old English Household Life*, Batsford.

Kurella, E 1999, *The Complete Guide to Vintage Textiles*, Schiffer.

Lavitt, W 1982, *American Folk Dolls*, Alfred A Knopf.

Nicholson, H 1998, *The Loving Stitch*, Auckland University Press.

Parker, R 1984, *The Subversive Stitch*, The Women's Press.

Simpson, T 1974, *The Sugarbag Years*, Alister Taylor Publishing.

Taylor, N M 1986, *The Home Front*, Government Printer.

The Big Book of Needlecraft undated, Odhams Press.

The Book of Good Housekeeping, 1948, The National Magazine Company Pty Ltd.

The New Zealand Official Yearbooks 1930–59, Government Printer.

The Pictorial Guide to Modern Home Needlecraft 1943, Odhams Press.

The Women's Institute of New Zealand 1940, *Tales of Pioneer Women*, Whitcombe and Tombs.

Truth Cookery Book 1957, Truth (NZ) Ltd.

Weldons Encyclopedia of Needlework undated, The Waverley Book Co.

Woman's Magazine Annual 1932, 1933, 1934, 1937, London.

Various editions of the following magazines (published 1930s–50s) were also referred to:

Britannia and Eve, Home, My Home, Needlework Illustrated, English Woman's Weekly, New Zealand Woman's Weekly, Wife and Home, Woman and Home, Woman's Journal.

PREVIOUS PAGE: **Chatelaine made from dressmaking fabric, probably 1920s–30s.**

LEFT: **Felt tape-measure holder, 1930s–40s.**

RIGHT AND OVERLEAF: **Details from felt workbags, 1930s–40s.**

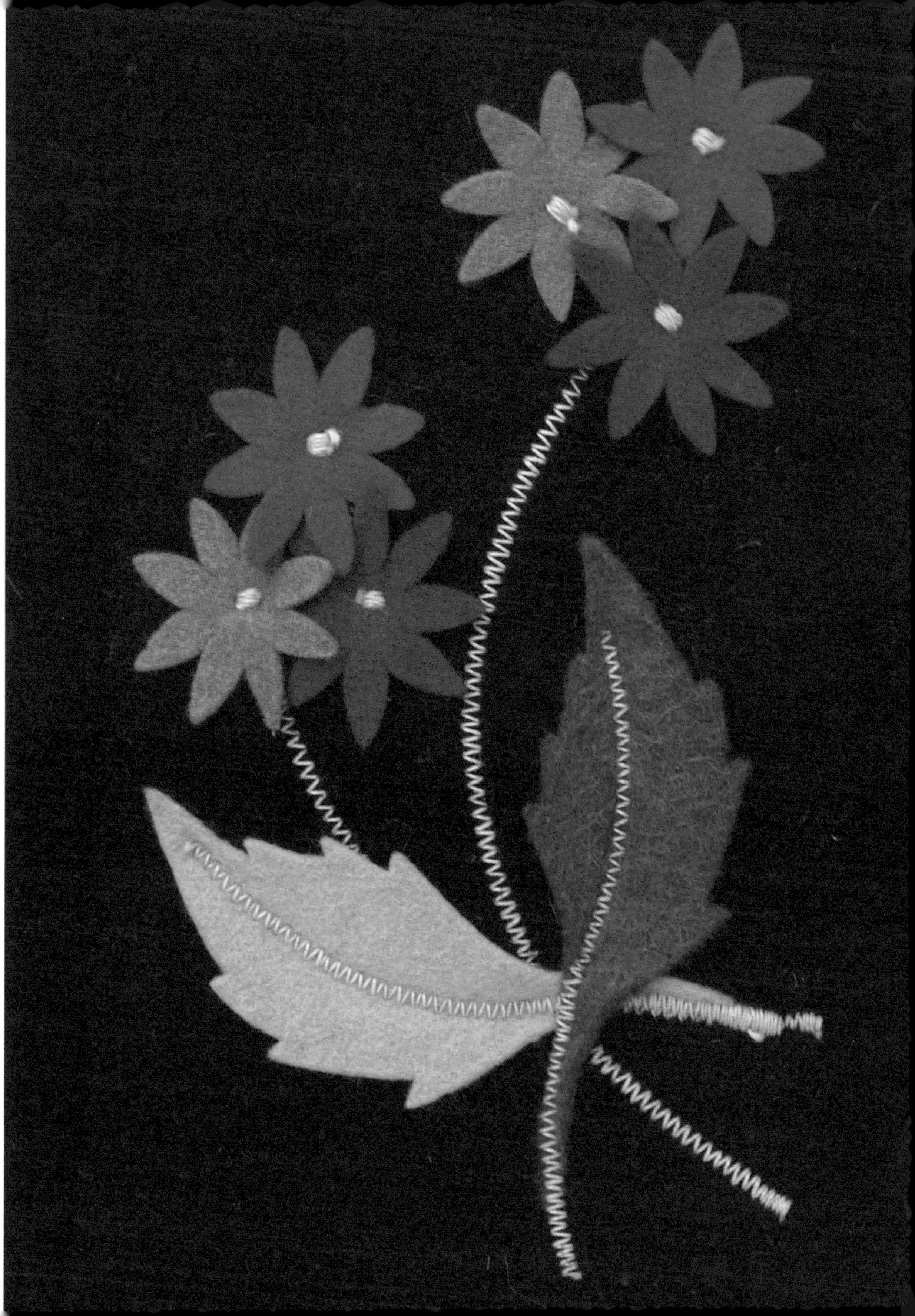